Crossings

Norwegian-American Lutheranism as a
Transatlantic Tradition

The Norwegian-American Historical Association

Lois M. Rand, President

BOARD OF PUBLICATIONS

Todd W. Nichol, Editor
Betty A. Bergland
Jon Gjerde
Ann M. Legreid
Terje I. Leiren
B. Lindsay Lowell
Deborah L. Miller
Orm Øverland
Janet E. Rasmussen
Clarence Burton Sheffield, Jr.

Crossings

Norwegian-American Lutheranism as a
Transatlantic Tradition

Edited by
Todd W. Nichol

Northfield, Minnesota
Norwegian-American Historical Association
2003

In memory of

Marion John Nelson

(1924–2000)

Contents

Preface

THE ARTICLES GATHERED HERE ORIGINATED in lectures presented to a conference on the history of Norwegian-American Lutheranism held in April 2000 at Luther Seminary in Saint Paul, Minnesota. The theme of this gathering was *Crossings: Norwegian-American Lutheranism as a Transatlantic Tradition.* This event had both commemorative and scholarly aspects. As a celebrative occasion, *Crossings* was one of several observances throughout the United States marking the 175th anniversary of the beginning of large-scale Norwegian immigration to the United States. The intellectual assignment for speakers and participants was twofold. The first purpose of their work was to discover what might be learned by studying comparatively the histories of two similar but distinct versions of the same religious tradition, Norwegian Lutheranism and Norwegian-American Lutheranism. Their second task was to explore the history of the exchange of influences between the Church of Norway and the Norwegian-American Lutheran churches in the United States.

These essays address specific topics and do not individually or as a whole purport to present a consensus on method or a new interpretative synthesis. They do, however, experiment with methods and set out lines of inquiry that may point the way toward a revised interpretation of Norwegian Lutheranism on both sides of the Atlantic. Five observations about the way method and material inform each other emerge quickly from a reading of these articles. First, and consistent with the theme of *Crossings,* several of these scholars adopt synoptic perspectives that keep both Europe and the United States in view at the same time. They demonstrate that from roughly 1850 on neither Norwegian Lutheranism nor Norwegian-American Lutheranism can be fully understood without taking the cognate tradition on the other side of the Atlantic into account. Second, a number of these writers also present evidence that there was for a century and more a lively exchange of influences across the Atlantic, however sporadic or interrupted this may from time to time have been. Third, without prior consultation each of these writers has turned to popular expressions of this tradition to explore its dynamics. In every case, the authors of these studies have either used hitherto largely unexplored material or they have looked at familiar data in new ways. Fourth, the use of diverse sources has required of these scholars an interdisciplinary approach to church history. They bring to this field a variety of methods already developed in other disciplines, including literary criticism, folklore, and art history. Fifth and perhaps most importantly, the use of material neglected by earlier church historians does more than complement existing narratives. It results in a fundamentally changed version of the history of Norwegian-American Lutheranism.

As a group these articles illustrate the wealth that awaits researchers who seek sources and adopt methods not traditionally used by church historians. Jon Gjerde, for example, sets the story of these churches in political and social contexts that help explain their internal histories more clearly than would be possible without the methods of the social historian. The same may be said of essays by Orm Øverland, Kathleen Stokker, and Marion John Nelson. In these instances, close textual analysis informed by both historical methods and a literary-critical approach, the techniques of folklore studies, and the skills of an art historian each make new insights possible. Articles by Bjørn Sandvik, Vidar L. Haanes, Øyvind T. Gulliksen, and Lloyd Hustvedt examine more familiar data, but ask freshly formulated questions and keep an eye on less familiar ancillary resources. Thus Sandvik is able to pierce through a venerable myth surrounding the practice of catechesis and propose a point of departure for reconsidering the history of the indoctrination of youth in both Norway and the United States. Haanes discusses how the rank and file of church folk and pastors in Norway attempted to take direction of the education of their pastors and then looks at ways their efforts were informed by similar undertakings in the United States. Gulliksen examines not textbooks in homiletics or the sermons of notable leaders, but sermons preached by a conventional minister and heard by a typical congregation. Hustvedt tells the story of a single congregation from the perspective of pew rather than pulpit.

These scholars make us acutely aware that the historians of Norwegian-American Lutheran church life, like church historians in general, have in the past tended toward a fairly restricted range not only of methods but of material. The result has been a sound but canonically narrow version of the story. The history of Norwegian-American Lutheranism has, in fact, often been told primarily in terms of its denominational, institutional, and theological elements. The lives of prominent ecclesiastics have likewise received considerable attention. It would, of course, be impossible to tell this story rightly without study of these topics, and there remains work still to be done in these areas. The work of the present essayists, however, makes it clear that the use of a greater range of methods and approaches will open new perspectives on the story of Norwegian-American Lutheranism. Inviting us as they do to attend more closely than we have in the past to the commonplaces and customs of ordinary members and congregations of the Norwegian-American Lutheran churches, these authors have already enlarged this history. Their work invites other contributions as well.

Marion John Nelson died just months after presenting his memorable lecture "Folk Art and Faith among Norwegian Americans" at the *Crossings* conference. This volume is dedicated to the memory of this humane and learned colleague.

Todd W. Nichol
St. Olaf College
Luther Seminary

Acknowledgments

MANY PEOPLE CONTRIBUTED to the preparation of this volume. Each of the essayists spoke in April 2000 at Luther Seminary, Saint Paul, Minnesota at the conference *Crossings: Norwegian-American Lutheranism as a Transatlantic Tradition.* All of them took account of the discussion that followed their presentations and later prepared the present articles for publication.

A number of colleagues at Luther Seminary gave valuable assistance in organizing and presenting the *Crossings* conference. Marc Kolden, Dean of Academic Affairs, provided support and resources to make the event possible. President David L. Tiede also lent counsel and took part in a portion of the program. Archivist Paul Daniels and Faculty Secretary Alice Loddigs assisted in planning and carrying out the program.

Following the untimely death of Marion John Nelson, Lila Nelson located the first draft of her husband's article and kindly consented to its publication. She, along with Clarence Burton Sheffield, Jr., assisted in editing the article and securing illustrations. Sylvia Ruud assisted in preparing the manuscript for publication and designed the dustjacket.

Professor Odd S. Lovoll of St. Olaf College provided encouragement when the idea of *Crossings* was germinating and more specific guidance along the way toward the conference and the publication of this volume. This was the last manuscript he accepted for publication before he retired as editor of the Norwegian-American Historical Association.

I thank all of these friends.

TWN

5 February 2003

Crossings

The Perils of "Freedom" in the American Immigrant Church

Jon Gjerde

"GO . . . OUT IN THE CONGREGATIONS," Gjermund Hoyme (1847–1902) wrote in 1888, "and look on the schism where the scornful laugh of Satan mixes with the death cries of the people as the billows of party strife clash the people against the rock of salvation only to have them fall again into the sea of their own agitation." In a scenario suggestive of the apocalypse, Hoyme asked his listeners to "go into the community" where one saw "the glances of Cain exchanged" as one heard "the church bells ring strife into the air."[1] Philip Schaff, writing three decades before, was more sanguine. "In the United States all nations, all churches and sects, all the good and evil powers of the old world, meet without blows or bloodshed; and while Europe began with paganism and barbarism, America begins with the results of Europe's two thousand years' course of civilization, and has vigor, energy, enterprise, and ambition enough to put out this enormous capital at the most profitable interest for the general good of mankind."[2] There is much to contrast in these two observations. One appears to be hopelessly pessimistic; the other is remarkably sanguine. One predicts apocalypse; the other a bloodless betterment of humankind. Although apparently contradictory, these two observations may be linked by a common theme. Both Hoyme and Schaff were reacting to the environment of the United States that provided a new religious context, both challenging and

3

exhilarating, for the practitioners of varied European religious traditions. Here I will focus on the opportunity—what contemporaries would have called the "freedom"—to replant their faiths in the United States.

I want first to show how immigrants from Europe and their religious leaders explicitly celebrated the American environment, which promised a freedom of religion in the nineteenth century. In fact, I contend that their attachment to the American state was fostered by this environment that enabled them to practice their beliefs, speak their language, and create institutions that were both European and American in orientation. These freedoms, however, were not without their price, as the second section of the essay will argue. Religious traditions were developing in Europe as they were being transplanted to the United States. Pietistic awakenings that coursed across Europe in the nineteenth century were matched by confessional movements that especially influenced Lutheranism, Anglicanism, churches of the Reformed tradition, and Roman Catholicism. When we focus on confessional traditionalism, we will observe how the freedoms of an increasingly liberal United States came into conflict with people who were leery of the outcomes of American liberalism.

The purported freedoms of the United States thus occasioned quandaries for many immigrant religions. They also created challenges for both clergy and laity when churches based on voluntary membership were formed and when the church was dependent on the laity for its sustenance rather than on the state. Whereas many such as Schaff could celebrate the liberating aspects of a church free of state interference, others such as Hoyme could observe outcomes of those freedoms that included theological strife. Norwegian-American Lutherans like Hoyme, perhaps more than the people of most immigrant religious traditions, puzzled over how the freedoms of the United States were to be folded into the developing beliefs in Europe and the United States. For them, as much as for other groups, the church bells could and did ring strife into the air.

AMERICAN FREEDOM AND THE "COMPLEMENTARY IDENTITY"

To understand the intertwining of relationships between religion, immigration, and the state in the United States, we must begin by considering some basic structures of American government encoded into law by the Constitution. First, while the First Amendment provides for the freedom of religion, the founders were careful not to create an established or "state" church. The men who drafted the Constitution were fully aware of the religious wars that had spread across Europe in the previous centuries and of the religious pluralism that existed in their new nation. Whether their intent was to protect the state from religion or vice versa, they separated the church from the state and concluded that freedom of religion was an inalienable right.

Second, Congress enacted generous laws of naturalization and citizenship for people defined as "white," a category that corresponded to immigrants of European ancestry. In the United States, citizenship was based on *jus soli,* that is, people born in the country were citizens by law. Still, as early as 1790, the United States Congress adopted a liberal naturalization policy that enabled immigrants to be naturalized after two years' residence in the nation, a requirement that later would be lengthened to five years.[3]

European immigrants were thus entitled both to relatively easy access to American citizenship and to freedom of religion. This conjunction of the opportunity to be both members of a body politic and of a church was often received with optimism by clergy and laity alike in the nineteenth century. European church leaders frequently praised religious freedom as a hallmark of American life that actually strengthened the church. Schaff, quoting Luther's observation that "faith is a free thing, which can be forced on no one," wrote that "the civil equality of all churches and sects in America, and the voluntary system inseparable from it, have aroused and are sustaining a great mass of individual activity." Schaff contended that "the United States are by far the most religious and most Christian country in the world . . . because religion there is most free." H. A. Preus, a Norwegian-American Lutheran pastor, framed the issue in gendered terms when speaking in Oslo twenty years later. Norwegian-American Lutheranism, he assured his audience, was "like a more vivacious daughter . . . not as demure and considerate as her mother." Although this daughter "has some bad habits because she feels so free and is not yet used to her freedom," he continued, "she is still the inwardly beautiful bride of Christ." Others compared this vivacity to the more staid European churches. C. F. W. Walther, a leader among German-American Lutherans, contended that "we live here in a State in which the church enjoys a freedom unsurpassed since its origin, and at present to be found scarcely anywhere else in the world. . . . We have here full liberty to regulate everything according to God's Word and the model of the church in its best days and to give our church a truly Christian and apostolic form." Walther concluded, "if we take a glance at our old German Fatherland, how entirely different do we find it! There the church is bound in chains."[4]

This sense of "liberty" was a critical dimension in areas of immigrant life other than the practice of religion. Because immigrants were residents with rights of citizenship, their leaders were forced to balance the development of the ethnic and religious group with that of integration into membership in the nation. Immigrants who became ethnics thus not only created myths of belonging that fostered an ethnic identity, but they also merged their particularistic stories into larger narratives of nation. In so doing, they were central actors in creating what I will call "complementary" identities that fused a variety of multi-leveled identities in relation to one another.[5] As I will define it, the complementary identity merges allegiance to national and ethnic or religious groups in a self-reinforcing dynamic that embeds pluralism into the national fabric as immigrants and their leaders understand it. This ingenious construction, however, had its risks for ethnic leaders: membership in the nation could come to threaten both the fervency of religious belief and the content of church teaching.

Complementary identity was fostered when ethnics and immigrants in the nineteenth-century United States combined both a concern for their place in the new country and a sense of a common past on the basis of which they created a common ethnic group. For this perspective, they needed to merge the myths of the United States with those of their group. They quickly became aware that residents of the United States in the nineteenth century celebrated the many ways in which their republic improved upon the tired systems of the old European states. Introduced as they were to the rhetoric and institutions of American exceptionalism by their leadership, immigrants tended to celebrate the American political and social system itself. Mid-nineteenth-century European immigrants commonly praised the economic possibilities that defined the nation. They were also predisposed to esteem the nation's political institutions with their "natural freedom and equality." These identifications were powerful forces in encouraging recent arrivals to develop loyalties to the United States and to learn about its institutions.

A few examples of this rhetoric might give an indication of its content. Noting that the American government was unhampered by monarchical and aristocratic interests, Norwegian Johan R. Reiersen argued in 1843 that there was created a "spirit of progress, improvements in all directions, and a feeling for popular liberty and of the rights of the great masses exceeding that of any land in Europe." As a result, republican government would not fail, in large part because "the masses" would never be "reduced—through the power of individuals or of capital—to the same slavish dependence that supports the thrones of Europe. Personal freedom is something the people suck in with their mother's milk," he concluded. "It seems to have become as essential to every citizen of the United States as the air he breathes. It is part of his being, and will continue to be until his whole nature is cowed and transformed in the bondage of need and oppression."[6] The letters from a Norwegian correspondence society of immigrants likewise stressed the spirit of freedom in the United States which, they maintained, contained "the secret of general equality."[7] A German immigrant, writing to his kin in Europe at about the same time, compared his former home to his new one. In Germany, "alas, common sense and free speech lie in shackles," he wrote. If his relatives wished "to obtain a clear notion of *genuine* public life, freedom of the people and sense of being a nation," he contended, they should emigrate. "I have never regretted that I came here, and never! never! again shall I bow my head under the yoke of despotism and folly."[8] Other immigrants, although writing in a different language, used nearly the identical imagery: Norwegians, they wrote, enjoyed tasting "the satisfaction of being liberated from the effect of all yoke and despotism."[9] Decades later, American "freedom" remained a trope for Germans explaining their forebears' migration to the United States. "Discontent prevailed in all classes of German society," wrote R. Puchner. "There was a longing for free political and free religious ideas; the old institutions seemed rotten and sick unto death; there was . . . only the ocean in between them [and] the new land of promise, the mighty republican Empire of America."[10]

The absorption of national myths, however, did not mean that European leaders discarded cultural pasts. On the contrary, they seized on common national, linguistic, and religious traditions as cornerstones for fashioning their ethnic collectivities. These ethnic groups created boundaries, oftentimes reconfiguring common pasts, that were instrumental for ethnic leaders in the pluralist society.[11] Ethnic institutions, based on common intellectual, geographical, or linguistic pasts originating in Europe, were created in the United States to support interest group associations in the polity and society. Nor did this process of "ethnicization" nullify the development of loyalties to the United States. Rather than competing, the dual loyalties to nation and subgroup, invented under the auspices of an American creed, could be complementary.[12]

The ideological underpinnings of citizenship that privileged "freedom" and "self-rule" in fact enabled immigrants to nurture simultaneously their bond to nation and to ethnic subgroup. Tropes of "freedom" and "liberty," perhaps because their meaning was so pliant, proved to be concepts that fostered an appreciation among immigrants of the responsibilities and rights of American citizenship. This frame of reference was used by immigrants to write their own myths of foundation even before the United States was a nation-state. In 1764, Christopher Saur, a Philadelphia German-American, would write: "whether you are Englishmen, Germans, Low-Germans or Swedes, whether you are of the High Church, Presbyterians, Quakers, or of another denomination, by your living here and by the law of the land you are *free men, not slaves*."[13] And Henry Miller, in a patriotic litany penned shortly before the Declaration of Independence was signed, reminded his readers, "Remember—and remind your families—you came to America, suffering many hardships, in order to escape servitude and enjoy liberty; Remember, in Germany serfs [*leibeigene*] may not marry without the consent of their master. . . . They are regarded as little better than black slaves on West Indian Islands."[14] A pliant use of the abstraction of freedom, set in a context of the unfreedom of the European world, thus was a useful rhetorical device for understanding life in the American republic.

Yet the very concept of freedom could also nurture the maintenance of old-world ties. One sense of "freedom," after all, implied a liberty to maintain patterns of life and practice conventions that varied from those of native-born Americans. Immigrants became citizens of the United States and performed their obligations as citizens, but basic rights inherent in their citizenship status allowed them to retain ethnic and religious allegiances carried from Europe. Immigrants and their children, then, could simultaneously, in a complementary, self-reinforcing fashion, maintain allegiances to the United States and to their former identities outside its borders.

In this way, faithfulness to an ethnic subgroup within a "complementary identity" theoretically fostered a magnified loyalty to the United States. Ethnic allegiances encouraged affinities with nation. As Samuel P. Huntington has argued, "defining and maintaining an ethnic identity was an essential building block in the process of creating an American national identity."[15] An ideologically based national identity, on the other hand, enabled people to reformulate former beliefs and to foster the formation of ethnic groups in the United States. In its stable form, then, the complementary identity was more than the opportunity to develop a dual identity within nation and ethnic subgroup: it was a self-reinforcing concept that powerfully promoted an allegiance to American institutions at the same time that it fostered a maintenance of ethnic forms. Pluralism was embedded within national loyalty.

Evidence from memoirs and newspapers indicates that mid-nineteenth-century immigrants almost intuitively understood this complementarity. "Americanization" typically had a very different meaning for the myriad ethnic communities in the United States than it did for American-born nativists.[16] The editor of *Den Swenske Republikanen* in 1857, for example, argued that his paper indeed intended to "Americanize" its readers, which to him meant "to acquaint them with the republican institutions of America and make those institutions respected and loved."[17] They could be loyal citizens of the United States and members of ethnic groups simultaneously. Those from many nations found it simple to translate Carl Schurz's advice to his male German counterparts: "I love Germany as my mother, America as my bride."[18]

Ethnic Americans throughout the nineteenth century ingenuously conflated these multiple loyalties. Public celebrations of national holidays, for example, consolidated images of the European past and the American present. Irish celebrated the Fourth of July in 1883 and merged it with advocacy of the Land League and of independence for Ireland.[19] Swiss-Americans saw no incongruity in merging the history of Switzerland into their Fourth of July observance in 1876. Their centennial parade float contained representations of Helvetia and Columbia surrounded by images of the Swiss cantons with their coats of arms.[20] A German rural community six years later celebrated American life by reading the Declaration of Independence and listening to a speaker discuss the German role in support of the Revolutionary War, "a role," reported a German-language newspaper, "too little known."[21] "The jewels of Isabella the Catholic," Bishop John Hughes reportedly observed, "would be an appropriate ornament for the sword of Washington."[22] Some years later, Cardinal James Gibbons, upon watching the American and papal flags carried side by side at a parade, observed that "I always wish to see those two flags lovingly entwined, for no one can be faithful to God without being faithful to his country."[23] And Roman Catholic newspaper mastheads juxtaposed portraits of George

Washington and Pope Pius X, a clear illustration of the importance and compatibility of allegiance to both church and state.[24]

EUROPEAN RELIGIOUS ORIGINS

These encounters with "freedom" created challenges for the religious communities being built by European immigrants. Most obviously, a church free of state interference was also a church that needed to sustain itself. Congregations and synods had to devise ways to fund church buildings and remunerate their clergy. Another less obvious but perhaps more perplexing dilemma was the challenge of balancing allegiance to state and church. Although they typically celebrated the freedom to practice their beliefs, religious leaders often feared that these very freedoms might also propagate a license among their flock that would erode central beliefs that knit them together. To understand more fully these challenges, we must consider the European roots of the religious traditions transplanted to the United States.

Immigrant religious communities in the nineteenth-century United States were profoundly influenced by contemporary European intellectual movements that evolved in reaction to the excesses during decades of revolution and upheaval and to the sterile rationalism and formalism of the Enlightenment. One expression was a flourishing pietistic opposition that encouraged emotionally charged spiritual awakenings among the peasantry in Europe, as it did in the United States.[25] Significantly, this pietist sentiment was rerooted in the United States by European immigrants who, in many cases, were able to fuse their religious convictions with social and political perspectives consonant with American Protestantism. As Timothy L. Smith argues, this was crucial to the development of "modern" goals, including autonomy and self-realization, which in turn contributed to the mobilization of the peoples that would comprise European immigration.[26] As such, these religious groups were able to integrate their churches into the political landscape of the United States.

In contrast, this European pietism was accompanied and often opposed by a flourishing religious culture beginning in the early nineteenth century that was not so "modern." If pietism was one avenue to protest the barren rationalism of the eighteenth century, there also was a reawakening of theological themes that not only had dominated prior to the Enlightenment, but in many cases disparaged it.[27] The significance of these movements has often been lost, or at the very least understated, in United States history. Scholars have tended not to problematize immigrant religious thought, have assumed its liberal character, and have failed to perceive as a result the significance of varied religious bodies moving toward more confessional and corporatist postures during the period.

One is struck, in fact, by a similar sequence among many religious traditions transplanted to the United States. Religious principles that tended to be more liberal and ecumenical initially were repeatedly overlaid by movements that were more confessional, particularist, and corporatist. Among Roman Catholics, the Irish-American clergy who dominated the American Catholic hierarchy in the nineteenth century were not the principal advocates of Catholic corporatism but rather were instrumental in promoting a liberal or "Americanist" perspective aimed at transforming ethnics into "Americans." The strongest proponents of a conservative, corporatist Catholicism, on the other hand, were Continental members of the Church.[28] Deeply influenced by the corporatism espoused by Roman Catholics in the nineteenth century and later stung by the German Kulturkampf, German Catholics in the United States, as Philip Gleason has shown, hewed to a Christian order of society based on its "natural" institutions. At the same time, they eschewed forces in the United States such as liberalism, socialism, and anarchism that they perceived to be individualistic, materialistic, and atheistic. Divisions within the church would come to a head in the late nineteenth century when the conservative wing, which comprised the majority of the laity, confronted the liberal "Americanist" advocates.[29]

Immigrant Lutheranism and Calvinism followed a similar sequence from midcentury onward. Whereas the Lutheran church in the United States had gravitated toward liberal positions known as "American Lutheranism" in the early nineteenth century, its drift was arrested in part by the Lutheran German immigration at mid-century. Confessional German Lutheran leaders left Europe because they saw "no possibility of retaining" their "pure and undefiled" faith of the Lutheran confessions and thus sought a country "where this Lutheran faith is not endangered."[30] German-American church bodies that formed out of this immigration—Buffalo Synod (1845), Missouri Synod (1847), Wisconsin Synod (1850), and Iowa Synod (1854)—reestablished a confessional Lutheranism in the Middle West.[31] Scandinavian Lutherans, although they proved less inclined to accept particularist and corporatist thought than Germans, nonetheless were influenced by it.[32] Similarly, the first wave of Dutch immigrants in the nineteenth century maintained a pietism that had been expressed in the secession from the National Reformed Church in Holland in 1834.[33] Yet again, these beliefs were overlaid by another wave of migration in the late nineteenth century whose theology was deeply colored by a Dutch Calvinist corporatism based on the thought of Abraham Kuyper, which lamented the course of events and development of thought in the post-revolutionary age.[34]

To be sure, these developments were accompanied by shifts in the United States that reinforced a corporatist ideal. Catholic convert Isaac Hecker, for example, argued that the Roman Catholic Church was "a visible organic body instituted by Christ to teach those Divine Truths, and convey that Divine Life to men, which moved Him to come down from heaven, and unite His Godhead to our manhood in one personality in the flesh." Protestantism, he continued, erred because it was "the exaggeration of the authority of private judgment to the entire exclusion of all other authorities."[35] Fellow convert Orestes Brownson, using a romantic reference to the medieval world, agreed. "The chief thing we admire in the middle ages," he wrote, "is that men did then believe in God, they did believe in some kind of justice [and] that man did, whatever his condition, owe some kind of duty to his fellow man."[36]

These movements contained two strains of thought that would influence many European and American religious communities in the United States. The first was a tendency toward a particularism that reaffirmed the belief that one's particular religious confession and Scripture represented the one true faith. Among Protestants, this outlook was related to a confessional revival in the mid-nineteenth century that stressed that Scripture and confessions were immune from literary criticism. Within the hierarchy of the Roman Catholic Church, it found expression in a series of papal proclamations anti-liberal in character. In 1864, the publication of the *Syllabus of Errors* seemed to place the Roman Catholic Church in opposition to the secularism and liberalism of the century. Six years later, the Vatican Council accepted papal infallibility.[37] These particularist tendencies complicated believers' attempts to integrate religious belief into a national community that contained non-believers. Even when they accepted and celebrated the American state, many continued to puzzle over its relationship with their confessional community. If those who confessed a particular theology were the only godly folk in society, how ought they interact with the heathen?[38]

The second tendency was toward a renewal of a corporatist theology that tended to support institutional structures such as a hierarchical family as it opposed the premises on which liberalism was based. Corporatist theory, which influenced Roman Catholic and Protestant traditions alike, was built upon organic conceptions of state and society that assumed that comparisons between the body or the organism and the politically organized community were informative.[39] Roman Catholic natural law assigned a place in the whole for every being, and every link is based on a divine decree.[40] Individuals, knit into a societal whole, were further constrained by the privileged position given to "natural" institutions such as the family, the church, and occupational organizations such as the guild. Enmeshed in this web of institutions, they were obliged to consider the influences of these myriad interests rather than simply their relationship with the state. These institutions were not only "natural"; they tended to be societally ascribed. Human beings were not able to choose their parental relationships as they would membership in a voluntary organization. They were born into them.[41] Among Lutherans, grace within the spiritual community was contrasted with the rule of law and coercion in the secular one. Religion itself thus remained a matter of faith rather than of law. The irrational state was surfeited with power, and the believer's place in the world—his or her "calling"—was established on "a system of perfect sublimation of social function in a given static order."[42] Abstract political equality within society did not exist; there was only a functional equality in the form of occupational worth. As in Roman Catholic belief, society was "not an aggregate but an organism."[43]

The dilemma was thus clear: although many church leaders celebrated the freedoms of the American republic, they simultaneously were concerned that individual freedoms in a liberal republic were a potential threat to proper societal structures. At the very least, many of them worried that the increasingly liberal tone in nineteenth-century American society could create a society of excess, materialism, and individualism.[44] Ironically, they valued the freedom that permitted people to reestablish communities of belief in America, but they feared the logical outcome when those within the communities also claimed their individual freedoms. For what if an individualism that grew out of liberalism was valued in society and polity yet was inadvisable in family life, community structures, or religious belief? And how were some freedoms acceptable whereas others were to be rejected? They were well aware in the early nineteenth century of what Walter Lippman would later term the "acids of modernity."[45] In this sense religious leaders were concerned that their people might lose track of what they themselves considered the real purpose of existence on this earth.

THE PERILS OF "FREEDOM" IN THE AMERICAN IMMIGRANT CHURCH

The tensions and contradictions between some immigrant religious traditions and the conditions of American life created a variety of challenges for residents of the United States in the nineteenth century. One result, which we will not consider in depth, was the purported impact of various church traditions on the future of the United States. A common portrayal of Roman Catholicism in the United States, for example, was focused on its tendency toward tyranny and "unfreedom" that would undermine the American republic. Rather than viewing the ways in which religious faiths undermined American freedom, we will now turn our attention to the ways in which American freedom challenged the direction of the church. In sum, we will see how "freedom" was a double-edged sword for the clergy who accepted many of the premises of American liberty but found that it fundamentally contradicted the ways in which they understood the world.

First, if the freedoms were currently beneficial for the church, what would be their long-term consequences? On some levels, the clergy feared the excesses of freedom. H. A. Preus thus could express his admiration for the American republic at the same time that he confessed a fear of "men who embraced a false humanism and were intoxicated with the modern rage for 'natural and inalienable human rights,' who considered outward, temporal freedom *absolutely* necessary to human beings."[46] Samuel Mazzuchelli, a pioneer priest in Wisconsin, would certainly have nettled Preus when he argued that "Protestantism has degenerated into a purely negative doctrine founded on *individual caprice and understanding,* influenced by every human passion and frailty." Yet Preus might have agreed with his conclusion that "in America, where the spirit of personal independence is carried to the extreme," individual understanding and sectarian competition turned into a mean-spirited popularity contest. "Sectarians," Mazzuchelli argued, "are even more disposed to deny what others believe, in order to give free rein to the suggestions of pride, malice, self-interest, passions, fanaticism, and *individual delusions.*" Truth was thus the ultimate loser, as "the authority and teachings of all the ages are laid low before the defective and fallacious reasoning of every sectarian with the proud exclamation, 'I am free!'"[47] Freedom and majority rule, proudly proclaimed in the political sphere, failed when they entered the sanctuary. Yet in the United States, "the political principle that the majority ought to rule," Mazzuchelli insisted, also regulated religious matters in every Protestant denomination. The maxim "I am free" thus extended beyond politics so that it became "the source of innumerable intellectual vagaries . . . which never hinder the public preaching of the most extreme religious doctrines."[48] When political freedoms diffused into the spiritual world, the concept of freedom became incongruous.

Protestant Europeans were not at ease either with what one Norwegian-American Lutheran clergyman called "these blooming vagaries about freedom."[49] Although Protestant sects shared an animosity towards the Church of Rome, they often feared the consequences of freedom of religion as well. European Protestant religious traditions, particularly in the more liturgical branches of the Lutheran and Reformed churches, also struggled with the many manifestations of what one writer called a "churchly confusion . . . in this land harrowed by so many erring sects," which followed directly from religious freedom.[50]

First, Protestant leaders grappled with a religious freedom that bred a disarray among sects and congregations. The wife of a Norwegian Lutheran pastor believed that two congregations under the leadership of her husband "were insane." "They want to build churches," she wrote, "but they are to be open to any odd tramp who wants to come and preach to them, and of these there are a large number in this country. . . . This is a free country, they say, and everyone can do as he pleases."[51] Second, an infatuation with democracy within the church could taint religious truth. If majority rule functioned in government, some argued that it could also be practiced in the church. Europeans, even those who were enamored with the Republic and the separation of church and state, expressed amazement that, as one put it, congregations were "given a formal right to act contrary to God's Word if it can merely summon a two-thirds majority for a decision."[52]

These concerns were not idle musings. Confusion between liberty and license, between authority and freedom, erupted in congregations throughout the nation. We may cite myriad religious traditions to illustrate this contention. Norwegian-American Lutheranism, however, provides some of the best examples, so this will be our focus as we return full circle to the quotation from Gjermund Hoyme that introduced this essay. The tensions between religious teachings and American church structures were often the grist for profound contention within the ethnic community. Whereas leaders frequently quarreled over the direction of the church and the freedoms and rights of the membership in the new American milieu, those within the community often argued with their leaders and bickered among themselves. The contention oftentimes pitted the leader against his flock. In a fictional account, a pastor recently arrived from Norway chastised his congregation for the inadequate welcome he had received from the community. His brief lecture did little to quell dissent. "And now there is one thing I will tell you . . . priest," replied a lay leader in a speech that encapsulates common perceptions of freedom in America, "and that is you had better not be as unyielding and haughty as the priests in the old country, for here it is the common man that rules, you see. Here we are in a free country, you see, and the bondage we struggled under there, is at an end here in America, you see. And here we have no treasury that will pay you, so, nor any king or bishop to tell us we must do so and so. It is we farmers that steer the ship around here, you see. And if you don't want to bend to our liking, then it will be worse for yourself, for then you will find yourself starving on a rock pile. And then we would send you home again at your own expense. But if you are good and go on sensibly, as a proper pastor should, I know that folks are not a bit worse here than other places, and they will do what is right for all of you, big and small."[53] Another Norwegian parishioner was more succinct after his pastor warned his flock that he had been called by the Almighty: "We are the ones who are paying him," he observed, "not the Almighty."[54] In both cases, the lesson was simple: if the congregations paid the pastor's salary, he was an employee who would face reprimands if he did not adequately perform his duties, a judgment paradoxically to be made by people who were at once members of his congregation and his employers.

If the congregation could choose its leadership, it might follow and it sometimes did that questions of church law and doctrine could also be resolved by majority rule. As one man, amid a religious controversy, argued simply in O. E. Rølvaag's novel *Peder Victorious*: "In all democratic organizations the majority ruled; it had to be so, or there would be anarchy."[55] Historical events mirrored historical fiction. During intense debate over predestination in 1885, for example, a congregation called for a vote to settle the matter. The pastor objected, asking rhetorically, "How could a majority determine what was God's law?" The congregation considered his protest, but a vote was taken nonetheless. Its members contended that the ministry did not necessarily possess any greater insight than the congregation into the interpretation of God's law and that perhaps the wisdom of the majority would come as close to the truth as possible. One member was bold enough to suggest that the pastor, because he opposed the vote, was a "false teacher."[56]

Issues of voluntary membership and democratic representation in secular and spiritual matters that divided leadership and laity tended to cleave congregations as well. Two controversies, which I cannot explore in detail, illustrate conflict that split congregations and divided layfolk from ministers. They also show how the perils of freedom intruded in myriad ways into questions of faith. The first dispute revolved around divisions in the Norwegian Synod among the clergy and between some of the clergy and laity over the question of slavery amid the Civil War.[57] Norwegian immigrants, who tended to be members of the Republican party, were schooled in anti-slavery ideologies by their political leaders. So, many members of the Norwegian Synod were bemused when it came to light in 1861 that leading clergy had drafted a ministerial declaration that argued that slavery "in and by itself" was not a sin. Whereas the laity viewed slavery as a contemporary issue connected to the disgusting behavior of slaveholders, secession, and fratricidal civil war, these clergymen saw slavery as a timeless doctrinal issue. For the latter, the issue was related to distinctions between temporal and spiritual freedom and ultimately to the validity of Scripture. In this debate that divided clergy from one another and from their parishioners, doctrinal authority came into conflict with a tidal wave of contemporary public opinion. Amid an agonizing debate, the clergy were forced to contemplate the meaning of freedom and slavery in contemporary America as interpreted in relation to timeless Christian truths.

The second controversy was the controversy over predestination that divided the Norwegian Synod in the 1880s. We need not venture into the fine theological distinctions that divided Norwegian Lutherans in the United States. Suffice it to say that there developed a division concerning the nature of God's predestination. The orthodox view argued that predestination and thus salvation itself was based solely on God's electing grace. Opponents argued that God grants salvation in view of the faith (*intuitu fidei*) to which he knows believers will by grace come. This conflict is notable for us for two reasons. First, an issue that seems rather abstract and obscure deeply divided Norwegian communities and churches. As one man wrote, "they argued predestination in the saloons with their tongues, and settled it in the alley with their fists."[58] Whether or not fisticuffs could solve this complex issue, congregations also divided over it. Upwards of one-third of the pastors and congregations withdrew from the Norwegian Synod as a result of the conflict.[59] Research I have conducted has suggested that this theological issue was a catalyst that fostered divisions of class and regional background.[60] Complicated theological issues, in short, animated Norwegian immigrants and their children in a most profound way. The fact that they were invested in debating and attempting to solve theological questions must have been related in some way to their new role as actors in church issues in the United States.

Second, issues of freedom cut to the heart of the controversy. It was likely not lost on the parishioners that church doctrine in the putatively freer environment of the United States had shifted theologically toward what could be construed as a less egalitarian position with regard to salvation. Like the slavery controversy that had erupted two decades before, the predestination controversy can be linked to attempts to retain orthodoxy in a clamorous new environment. It was a debate that could seem to favor abstract expressions of grace in a setting that rejected such abstractions, especially if they smacked of some denial of human freedom. And it was these divisions that induced Gjermund Hoyme to contemplate an apocalypse.

CONCLUSION

The situation was probably not as bad as Hoyme thought it to be. The death cries of people who were being dashed against the rock of salvation were probably rare in the Norwegian Lutheran church congregations that dotted the American landscape. In fact, clergy of many confessions through it all remained optimistic about the future.

For H. A. Preus, the free church permitted every activity to be "directed according to God's Word." Pastors in such a setting were not "hemmed in by the prejudices, constraints, and burdens of the state church."[61] For Philip Schaff, a leader of the Mercersburg movement, what he called the "present distraction and fermentings of Protestantism" were the necessary condition that would ultimately lead to Christian unity. "Protestantism," he argued, "will continue to dissolve into sects and parties, till it reduces itself to atoms, and thus, wearied with the endless fluctuation of subjectivity, and longing for repose in some tangible infallible authority, negatively prepares itself to return into the bosom of the one unchangeable Catholic church."[62] And for Samuel Mazzuchelli, Catholic writers "whose pens are never idle" could attack the errors of Protestantism and fanaticism. With superior logic, Catholic pens would force "the followers of error" either to "submit and profess the truth or else, rejecting every religious system whatsoever, abandon themselves to unbelief which is, in its effects, little different from paganism."[63]

Ultimately, such unity was not to be. In fact, what Schaff called the "sect system" has remained in place. The perils of freedom, moreover, remained a puzzle for church leaders who strove for Christian unity or who were disturbed at the excesses of Americans who seemed to mistake freedom for liberty. And it was especially so for those who, as they attempted to rejuvenate confessional forms of belief in the United States, ran smack up against a system that seemed to privilege Arminian beliefs. American religion continues to be a fractious enterprise and church leaders continue to be perplexed about the relationships between the sacred and secular worlds. Yet the perils of freedom were accompanied by the refuge that American religious freedom sanctioned. It might be argued that the church schisms in fact allowed for the creation of synods and congregations that were perhaps more responsive to parishioners' needs. Members of church congregations, moreover, were allowed to oppose their clergy if they felt they were in error. All this certainly can be related in some way to the fact that the United States is one of the most widely churched nations in the world, a fact that Schaff noticed already in the middle of the nineteenth century. And the opportunity

to build and rebuild religious communities without state interference continues to provide church members and their leaders the
chance to create religious environments that accord more with their
beliefs. In the end, these continuing conflicts within the church created, and continue to create, dilemmas for a significant group of church
leaders in the United States—the country that offered them religious
refuge, changed their religious belief and practice, and illustrated
the perils of freedom.

NOTES

[1]Gjermund Hoyme, "Aabningstale ved Fællesmødet i Willmar,
Minn., 1888," in *Efterladte Papirer,* ed. E. Kr. Johnsen (Minneapolis, 1904),
114–115. Hoyme's penchant for Victorian prose should not mislead the
reader as to his own assessment of the situation. He was famously optimistic about the possibility that Norwegian-American Lutherans could
overcome their divisions.

[2]Philip Schaff, *America: A Review of the Political, Social, and Religious
Character of the United States of America, in Two Lectures* (New York, 1855),
xviii.

[3]On this fact, see Rogers M. Smith, *Civic Ideals: Conflicting Visions of
Citizenship in U.S. History* (New Haven, 1997). The literature on immigration and naturalization law regarding Asian immigrants is particularly
rich. See, for example, Lucy E. Salyer, *Laws Harsh as Tigers: Chinese
Immigrants and the Shaping of Modern Immigration Law* (Chapel Hill, 1995);
and Charles J. McClain, Jr., *In Search of Equality: The Chinese Struggle
against Discrimination in Nineteenth-Century America* (Berkeley, 1994).

[4]Schaff, *America,* xii; Herman Amberg Preus, *Vivacious Daughter:
Seven Lectures on the Religious Situation among Norwegians in America,* ed.
and trans. Todd W. Nichol (Northfield, MN, 1990), 178. Walther is quoted
in Henry Eyster Jacobs, *A History of the Evangelical Lutheran Church in the
United States* (New York, 1893), 404.

[5]On the concept of "complementary identity," see Jon Gjerde,
*The Minds of the Midwest: Ethnocultural Evolution in the Rural Middle West,
1830–1917* (Chapel Hill, 1987), 59–66; Peter A. Munch, "In Search of Iden-

tity: Ethnic Awareness and Ethnic Attitudes among Scandinavian Immigrants, 1840–1860," in J. R. Christianson, ed., *Scandinavians in America: Literary Life* (Decorah, 1985), 1–24. See also David M. Potter, "The Historian's Use of Nationalism and Vice Versa," in *History and American Society* (New York, 1973), 74–75; and Morton Grodzins, *The Loyal and the Disloyal: Social Boundaries of Patriotism and Treason* (Chicago, 1956).

[6]Johan Reinert Reiersen, *Pathfinder for Norwegian Emigrants by Johan Reinert Reiersen,* ed. and trans. Frank G. Nelson (Northfield, MN, 1981), 176, 183.

[7]Lars Fletre, "The Vossing Correspondence Society of 1848 and the Report of Adam Lövenskjold," *Norwegian-American Studies* 28 (Northfield, MN, 1979), 267.

[8]August Blümner to his relatives, 3 April 1838, in Walter D. Kamphoefner et al., eds., *News from the Land of Freedom: German Immigrants Write Home* (Ithaca, 1991), 103. See also letters on 164, 307, 393, 427, 478, 481–482, 494, 585, 602.

[9]Fletre, "The Vossing Correspondence Society," 267.

[10]R. Puchner to Kate Everest, New Holstein, Calumet County, 1890. Kate Levi papers. State Historical Society of Wisconsin archives.

[11]See Victor Greene, *For God and Country: The Rise of Polish and Lithuanian Ethnic Consciousness in America, 1860–1910* (Madison, WI, 1975); Jonathan D. Sarna, "From Immigrants to Ethnics: Toward a New Theory of 'Ethnicization,'" *Ethnicity* 5 (1978), 370–378; and William L. Yancey et. al., "Emergent Ethnicity: A Review and a Reformulation," *American Sociological Review* 41 (1976), 391–403.

[12]The subgroup in the complementary identity, as I shall outline it, could refer to class and status identification. It is very important to note, however, that divisions at midcentury tended to be based on racial, religious, and ethnic terms. See Kathleen Conzen et. al., "The Invention of Ethnicity: A Perspective from the U.S.A.," *Journal of American Ethnic History* 12 (1992), 8.

[13]Christopher Saur, *Eine zu dieser Zeit höchstnöthige Warnung und Erinnerung an die freye Einwohner der Provintz Pennsylvanien,* cited in Willi Paul Adams, "The Colonial German-language Press and the American Revolution," in *The Press and the American Revolution,* ed. Bernard Bailyn and John B. Hench (Boston, 1981) 180. My emphasis.

¹⁴Henry Miller, *Staatsbote,* 9 March 1776, as cited in Adams, "The Colonial German-language Press," 209–210.

¹⁵Samuel P. Huntington, *American Politics: The Promise of Disharmony* (Cambridge, 1981), 27.

¹⁶Indeed, "Americans" were considered those of Anglo-Saxon background about whom the immigrants had varying opinions. "Americanization," from this perspective, was impossible.

¹⁷*Den Swenske Republikanen,* 21 August 1857.

¹⁸Carl Schurz, quoted by Joseph Schröder in *Verhandlungen der vierten allgemeinen Versammlung der Katholiken deutscher Zunge der Vereinigten Staaten von Nord-Amerika in Pittsburgh, Pa., Am 22, 23, 24 und 25 September, 1890* (Pittsburgh, 1890), 69–70, as cited in Colman Barry, *The Catholic Church and German Americans* (Washington, DC, 1953), 124. Father Goller extended the metaphor when he noted that immigrants "may still treasure in their hearts the sweet memories of childhood; for only the renegade can forget the mother that bore him." But "far more dearer to them than the memories of childhood is the strong and beautiful bride, Columbia, who taught them to walk erect on God's earth in the proud consciousness of manhood." See Barry, *The Catholic Church and German Americans,* 173.

¹⁹See, for example, *Die Iowa,* 12 July 1883.

²⁰*Dubuque National Democrat,* 16 March 1876.

²¹*Die Iowa,* 13 July 1882.

²²Thomas R. Whitney, *A Defense of the American Policy* (New York, 1856), 71. This quotation was intended to indict Hughes as one substituting "the mitre for our liberty cap" and blending "the crozier with the stars and stripes." Yet it also clearly indicates the attempts to fuse the symbols of America with those of Catholicism in order to augment the loyalties to both.

²³Cited in Dorothy Dohen, *Nationalism and American Catholicism* (New York, 1967), 114.

²⁴See Sister Mary DePaul Faber, "The Luxemburger Gazette, A Catholic German Language Paper of the Middle West, 1872–1918" (master's thesis, Catholic University of America, 1948), 31.

²⁵In Scandinavia, a pietist flame that had flared in the early eigh-

teenth century but had been tempered by clerical rationalism during the Enlightenment was rekindled by leaders who followed in later eras. Divisions within the National Reformed Church led to the secession in the Netherlands of over one hundred churches by pietists who objected to the "cold formal orthodoxy" of theological rationalism. A pietist revival, wrapped up in a German romanticism and nationalism, also occurred in Germany simultaneously with rancorous efforts to unite the Reformed and Lutheran churches. For developments in Sweden, see George M. Stephenson, *The Religious Aspects of Swedish Immigration: A Study of Immigrant Churches* (Minneapolis, 1932), 1–48; and G. Everett Arden, *Augustana Heritage: A History of the Augustana Lutheran Church* (Rock Island, 1963), 4–12. For Norway, see John T. Flint, *Historical Role Analysis in the Study of Religious Change: Mass Educational Development in Norway, 1740–1891* (Cambridge, 1990), 12–33; E. Clifford Nelson and Eugene L. Fevold, *The Lutheran Church among Norwegian Americans: A History of the Evangelical Lutheran Church,* 2 vols. (Minneapolis, 1960), 1:3–45. For German Lutherans, see J. L. Neve, *A History of Christian Thought,* 2 vols. (Philadelphia, 1946), 2:128–141; Heinrich H. Maurer, "The Problems of a National Church Before 1860," *American Journal of Sociology* 30 (1925), 534–550 and "The Problems of Group-Consensus: Founding the Missouri Synod," *American Journal of Sociology* 30 (1925), 665–682. For Holland, see Henry S. Lucas, *Netherlanders in America: Dutch Immigration to the United States and Canada, 1789–1950* (Ann Arbor, MI, 1955), 471–528; and James D. Bratt, *Dutch Calvinism in Modern America: A History of a Conservative Subculture* (Grand Rapids, 1984), 3–13.

[26]Timothy L. Smith, "Religion and Ethnicity in America," *American Historical Review* 83 (1978), 1165–1168.

[27]For a comparative overview of this confessionalist movement, see Walter H. Conser, Jr., *Church and Confession: Conservative Theologians in Germany, England, and America, 1815–1866* (Macon, GA, 1984).

[28]The best description of this ideology is found in Philip Gleason, *The Conservative Reformers: German-American Catholics and the Social Order* (Notre Dame, 1968). See also Barry, *The Catholic Church and German Americans.* French-Canadian Catholics, who lived mainly in the eastern United States, also advocated a Social Catholicism. See Gary Gerstle, *Working-Class Americanism: The Politics of Labor in a Textile City, 1914–1960* (New York, 1989), 247–250.

²⁹See Kerby A. Miller, *Emigrants and Exiles: Ireland and the Irish Exodus* (New York, 1985), 528–533, for an unsympathetic portrayal of the "conservatives"; and Jay P. Dolan, *The American Catholic Experience: A History from Colonial Times to the Present* (New York, 1985), 311–320, which notes that the conservative position was "the majority viewpoint among the rank-and-file clergy and laity."

³⁰A. R. Wentz, *A Basic History of Lutheranism* (Philadelphia, 1955), 116.

³¹For the history of this movement in the United States, see Theodore G. Tappert, ed., *Lutheran Confessional Theology in America, 1840–1880,* A Library of Protestant Thought, ed. John Dillenberger et al. (New York, 1972); and E. Clifford Nelson, ed., *The Lutherans in North America* (Philadelphia, 1975), 150–151.

³²Swedish immigrants gravitated toward pietistic expressions that led them to forsake Lutheranism in significant numbers, whereas Danish Americans were divided between pietists and adherents of N. F. S. Grundtvig, the great Danish nationalist theologian. It was within Norwegian Lutheranism that a corporatist formulation was advanced by the clergy and where major battles were fought between the leadership and their followers who questioned them. See Arden, *Augustana Heritage*; Jette Macintosh, *Danskere i midtvesten: Elk Horn-Kimballton bosættelsen 1870–1925* (Copenhagen, 1993), 102–129; Nelson and Fevold, *The Lutheran Church among Norwegian-Americans*; and Theodore C. Blegen, *Norwegian Migration to America: The American Transition* (Northfield, MN, 1940), 100–174, 241–276, 418–453.

³³See Lucas, *Netherlanders in America*; and Bratt, *Dutch Calvinism in Modern America.*

³⁴For Kuyper, the French Revolution attempted to "build up an artificial authority based on the free will of the individual" that "destroyed that organic tissue, broke those social bonds, and finally, in its work of atomistic trifling, had nothing left but the monotonous self-seeking individual, asserting his own self-sufficiency." Abraham Kuyper, *Christianity and the Class Struggle,* trans. Dirk Jellema (Grand Rapids, 1950), as cited in Bratt, *Dutch Calvinism in Modern America,* 23.

³⁵I[saac] T. Hecker, *Aspirations of Nature,* 4th ed. (New York, 1869 [1857]), 295–296, 307–308.

³⁶Orestes A. Brownson, "The Present State of Society," *Democratic Review,* July 1843, 41.

[37]For a brief overview, see Peter Steinfels, "The Failed Encounter: The Catholic Church and Liberalism in the Nineteenth Century," *Catholicism and Liberalism: Contributions to American Public Philosophy*, ed. R. Bruce Douglass and David Hollenback (Cambridge, 1994), 19–44.

[38]H. Richard Niebuhr, *The Social Sources of Denominationalism* (New York, 1929), is still useful on this topic.

[39]On European corporatist thought, see Ralph H. Bowen, *German Theories of the Corporative State with Special Reference to the Period 1870–1919* (New York, 1947); Matthew H. Elbow, *French Corporative Theory, 1789–1948: A Chapter in the History of Ideas* (New York, 1953). Corporatist theory was organicist first because the demands of the whole, in society as in a body, took precedence over its single parts, since the survival of a part (or individual member) was based on the continuation of the whole, whereas the whole could survive without certain constituent parts. Moreover, as some parts of the body were more important to the whole than others, so were people unequal in social—but, importantly, not in divine—worth. Hence an inherent social inequality in society *and* a corporatist and hierarchical organization of authority were natural. Organicist thought also concluded that a social body, like a living organism, must resolve internal conflicts peacefully and gradually and must maintain peace between its constituent parts. This theory thus regretted the perceived chaos of the nineteenth century as it rejected the inheritance of the individualism of the Enlightenment, the egalitarianism of the French Revolution, and the atomism of liberalism and Marxism.

[40]Otto von Gierke, *Political Theories of the Middle Ages*, trans. William Maitland (Cambridge, 1938), 22.

[41]On the many permutations of these principles, see Melvin J. Williams, *Catholic Social Thought: Its Approach to Contemporary Problems* (New York, 1950), 263–308.

[42]Society for Lutherans, wrote Heinrich H. Maurer, was "organized on the order of the patriarchal family; economically it was a natural economy, usufructuary manor, or a guildshop, held together by traditionalism and the fear of the Lord." Heinrich H. Maurer, "The Sociology of Protestantism," *American Journal of Sociology* 30 (1924), 268.

[43]Maurer, "The Sociology of Protestantism," 269–270.

[44]These ideas emanated from a broad array of church leaders. As noted earlier, groups within Scandinavian and German Lutheranism,

Dutch Calvinism, and Irish and German Catholicism evinced a suspicion of the rationalism and liberalism that were hallmarks of the Enlightenment. As the nineteenth century unfolded, increasingly powerful reactions were voiced by European church leaders in the United States. The literature is vast. But see Stephenson, *The Religious Aspects of Swedish Immigration*, 1–48; Nelson and Fevold, *The Lutheran Church among Norwegian Americans*, 1:3–45; Tappert, *Lutheran Confessional Theology in America, 1840–1880*; Heinrich H. Maurer, "The Problems of a National Church before 1860" and "The Problems of Group-Consensus: Founding the Missouri Synod"; Miller, *Emigrants and Exiles*, 492–568; Gleason, *The Conservative Reformers*; Bratt, *Dutch Calvinism in Modern America*, 3–13.

[45]Walter Lippman, *A Preface to Morals* (New York, 1929), 8.

[46]Preus, *Vivacious Daughter*, 166.

[47]Samuel Mazzuchelli, *The Memoirs of Father Samuel Mazzuchelli O. P.* (1844; Chicago, 1967), 283–284. My emphasis.

[48]Mazzuchelli, *Memoirs*, 284.

[49]J. W. C. Dietrichson wrote about *"disse velsignede frihedsgriller"* in *A Pioneer Churchman: J. W. C. Dietrichson in Wisconsin, 1844–1850*, ed. E. Clifford Nelson (New York, 1973), 143.

[50]J. W. C. Dietrichson as cited in Peter A. Munch, "Authority and Freedom: Controversy in Norwegian American Congregations," *Norwegian-American Studies* 28 (Northfield, MN, 1979), 15.

[51]Caja Munch to her parents, 31 May–1 June 1857, cited in *The Strange American Way: Letters of Caja Munch from Wiota, Wisconsin, 1855–1859*, ed. Helene Munch and Peter A. Munch (Carbondale, IL, 1970), 97.

[52]Preus, *Vivacious Daughter*, 150. In this context, Preus was criticizing the Scandinavian Augustana Synod that included both Swedes and Norwegians.

[53]Kristofer Janson, "A Buggy Priest," unpublished manuscript, trans. Oscar A. Christiansen, 4–5. Oscar A. Christiansen Papers, Minnesota Historical Society. The story was originally published in *Præriens Saga: Fortællinger fra Amerika* (Chicago, 1885).

[54]Gerhard Armauer Hansen, *Memories and Reflections*, trans. G. A. Hansen (Würzburg, 1976), 115.

[55]O. E. Rølvaag, *Peder Victorious* (New York, 1929), 59–60. This was especially true in the United States, Rølvaag continued, where "full free-

dom in all matters of faith, that's the inalienable right of a people! Oh, ho—so that was the idea: [The leader and majority of a church] intended to set up a state church and coerce people by force? . . . Did not the constitution of the land grant them full liberty? Did they not pay taxes to the government in order to have protection? Ought they consent to being shackled like slaves out here in the kingdom where they themselves had wrested from the wilderness."

[56]Fort Ridgely and Dale Lutheran Church Records, 1885, Archives of the Evangelical Lutheran Church in America in Chicago, Illinois.

[57]Among the best treatments of this episode is still Blegen, *Norwegian Migration to America: The American Transition,* 418-453, on which this paragraph is based.

[58]V. Koren, "Hvad den Norske Synode har villet og fremdeles vil," in *Samlede Skrifter,* ed. Paul Koren, 4 vols. (Decorah, 1912), 3:444.

[59]Nelson and Fevold, *The Lutheran Church among Norwegian Americans,* 1:254.

[60]Jon Gjerde, "Conflict and Community: A Case Study of the Immigrant Church in the United States," *Journal of Social History* 19 (1986), 681-697.

[61]Preus, *Vivacious Daughter,* 178.

[62]Schaff, *America,* xv, 234.

[63]Mazzuchelli, *Memoirs,* 185-186, 283-286, 300-303.

Religion and Church in Early Immigrant Letters: A Preliminary Investigation

Orm Øverland

"The Norwegian immigration before the Civil War has had a far greater in-fluence on the nationality's later development than one might believe by only looking at the relative numbers of those who came then and those who came later. Even though the latter are many times more in numbers, the first estab-lished and gave the still dominant tone to many important aspects of life."

—David Monrad Schøyen (1875)

"It is surely a great good from Providence that He has sent us so much of the benefits of this world that we may live in joy and happiness; but the greatest and most precious good is undeniably that we live in communion with God and His Holy Word, and of this we have had the most pleasant news from you. We both listen to and read many America letters, but most of them merely cry out about worldly matters and about what belongs to this life alone. Your letter has given us a truthful account of this as well as of the other, for which we thank you from our hearts."

—A letter from parents in Telemark to immigrants in Decorah, Iowa (May 1, 1852)

HISTORIANS MAY SEEM TO HAVE paid more attention to the early decades of Norwegian immigration than the numbers of people in-volved should dictate.[1] From 1825 to the end of the Civil War about

80,000 people came to the United States from Norway. In the following fifty years, from 1865 to 1915, the number is about 677,000. In the peak year of 1882 alone, almost 29,000 made the journey across the Atlantic. From many points of view the decades at the turn of the nineteenth century are of particular interest for studies in American immigration history. At no other time in American history have immigrants and their children made up so large a percentage of the population of the United States, and this had consequences both for the ways in which immigrants regarded themselves and the ways in which the native-born responded to immigrants and immigration.[2] Nevertheless, it may be said that the Norwegian immigrants who arrived at the turn of the nineteenth century could enter the already built structures of a Norwegian-American immigrant culture. This is certainly true of the immigrant Lutheran churches.

By 1860 the three main groupings in the 1917 merger that created the Norwegian Lutheran Church of America had been formed and may be traced through changing formal synodical structures. The Norwegian Synod and Hauge's Synod were in place by the early 1850s and the later United Church may be said to have had its beginnings in the Northern Illinois Synod and, at the end of the decade, in the Augustana Synod.[3] Since the history of the immigrant churches has largely been written from the perspective of theologically trained leaders and their many and often acrimonious doctrinal disputes, it may be that we have exaggerated the religious differences and not paid sufficient attention to the shared faith of the immigrants who made up the congregations of the various synods. Indeed, in emphasizing polarization in the study of Norwegian immigration by concentrating on the theological strife of church leaders and on the economic and social development of the immigrant population, it may also be that scholars have paid insufficient attention to the role of religion in the daily lives of the immigrants. The letters immigrants sent to relatives and friends in Norway are our most important source of knowledge about the experience of the individual men and women behind the statistics of migration. In my reading of a great many of these letters, most immigrants' thoughts about life were inseparable from their thoughts about an afterlife—just as most immigrants' concerns about economics, material improvement, and health were inseparable from their religious concerns. It is both the neglect of the latter and the consequent compartmentalization of the former that may give us a somewhat slanted picture of mid-nineteenth-century immigrants and their secular as well as their ecclesiastical institutions.[4]

Before looking at what immigrant letters may tell us of the role of religion in the lives of immigrants, we should note that immigrant letters of the early and mid-nineteenth century present challenges to present-day readers. The writers were, generally speaking, a remarkable group of people with quite exceptional resources of enterprise, character, and intellect. And yet they were often so untrained in writing that they were barely literate from our point of view. So how can we do justice to a literature by writers who had not learned to express themselves in writing and had no practice in the use of a pen? Some years ago I addressed this question and concluded that although the letters are "a rich and largely untapped store of human experience," their quality is only potential and depends on our ability to recreate this store of experience in our readings. This does not mean that we should add to the texts or make up for their deficiencies, but it does mean that our readings must try to realize the best intentions of the writers and recreate the urgency and the passion, the pain and the satisfaction of the immigrant experience.

When we pay special attention to religious expression in the letters, however, we are faced with the apparent paradox that, while the writers may lack the training or culture to write about their emotions or the beauty of the landscape, they seldom have a lack of words for religious sentiments. We must keep in mind that to the extent that these writers read at all, it was almost exclusively in religious texts. The only regular association they had with an educated use of language was in their churches where they listened to the learned expositions of their clergymen. It is therefore only natural that an intelligent but uneducated person could pick up this language and use it with some facility. So in assessing the importance of religion in the lives of mid-nineteenth-century immigrants it may also be necessary to consider the nature of the limited intellectual and cultural stimulation available to these writers. The facility with which many could write about religion may also make us exaggerate its importance.[5]

In our more secularized society religion is usually thought of not only as personal but as private. Since the personal letter is considered a private communication we may think of it as a natural place where religious faith may be displayed. Such a view, however, may lead to misreadings of mid-nineteenth-century immigrant letters, since such letters did not become private texts in our sense until the end of the 1860s when the new reorganization of the international postal system had taken effect. In the 1840s through most of the 1860s the price of a letter could vary from a standard 46 cents to two dollars or more depending on weight. In this period a woman could expect a wage of one to two dollars a week, while a man might get one dollar a day in the summer season or in the woods during the winter, but generally a good deal less. Letters were so expensive that they often were communal correspondences, involving several people on the writing side and being read or listened to by many people on the receiving side, so that expenses could be shared. In the letter sent from parents in Tinn in Telemark to their son and daughter-in-law in Iowa in 1852, quoted at the beginning of this article, they write that, "We both listen to and read many America letters." This should be taken quite literally in that these letters were read aloud to family and neighbors or were copied for futher distribution as public texts. Religious expression in immigrant letters is, according to my reading, largely personal but was certainly not private.[6]

Yet another preliminary question that has to be considered is the often-raised one of the reliability of these letters as sources. Among the many issues that must be kept in mind are those of representativeness. Here it is not merely a question of what kinds of immigrants tended to write but also of what kinds of families in Norway tended to preserve the letters so that they are available to us today. Questions of motivation, of the conditions under which the letters were written and those under which they were read, and of writing skills are only some of the many that must attend the historian's reading of immigrant letters.[7] In the following I will consider the role

and function of religion in the early immigrant letters in two different ways: first by reading one pioneer letter closely and then by sur-
veying a large selection that will at least be representative of the letters from the early period that have been preserved. Beginning with
the year 1847 and concluding with 1867 I will look at all letters for
every fifth year in the two first volumes of *Fra Amerika til Norge*.[8]

To illustrate the manner in which religious and secular concerns
are inseparable and to demonstrate that immigrants very quickly
freed themselves from an exaggerated respect for ecclesiastical authority without seeing themselves in conflict with divine authority, I will
first share with you a close reading of the first letter in the first volume
of the edition of immigrant letters I have co-edited with Steinar
Kjærheim. This is a letter written in Chicago by Svein Knudsen Lothe
to his brother in Hardanger on 10 July 1838.[9] As so often, the first thing
on the mind of this writer is his and his family's health, a crucial issue
in a situation where health spelled the difference between success and
calamity. However, his account of his and his wife's severe illness and
the doctor's pessimistic diagnosis moves quickly to reflections of a
transcendent nature: "It was not so good for us according to the ways
of the world but I hope and believe that it will be to our best. God the
Father be praised and thanked who has upheld me long enough that I
could learn to thank Him for it." In the next two sentences he writes
of missing his brother and urges him to come to Chicago.

He then describes the land from an agricultural point of view
and gives a quite detailed account of the price and procedure for the
acquisition of public land. In his matter-of-fact approach to spiritual as well as to secular concerns, to the life eternal as well as to trade
and business, he is of course in harmony with European Protestant
tradition in general and with the Norwegian Haugean movement in
particular. In this tradition Christian faith and trust in God does
not imply alienation from the temporal world but it may, as for this
writer, lead to a sober sense of the secondary importance of the latter. Indeed, this letter writer is so unquestioning of death as the passage from the temporal to the eternal and from a troubled life to the
good life that he probably smiled as he wrote down what he surely
thought was a good rhetorical stab at his implied opponent, the

bishop of Bergen, Jacob Neumann, who in 1838 had published a pamphlet warning peasants of the dangers of emigration.[10]

The ministers of the Norwegian state church were part of the country's governing elite of *embetsmenn,* the coterie of high-ranking civil servants that in a country without an aristocracy functioned as an upper class. In Norway the lay critique of the official ministry was naturally tempered by a respect for authority that might not be sanctified but was nevertheless sanctioned by God. This respect was for many no doubt weakened by the general tendency among church officials not only to speak against emigration but to do this from the pulpit. Nevertheless, in the Norwegian context the church largely retained its position among the laity as the sole administrant of the holy sacraments. With emigration, however, and the influence of American egalitarian attitudes, dissatisfaction with the ministry of the church could easily, as for this letter writer, develop into anti-clericalism. So accustomed have later generations become to an equation of the anticlerical with the antireligious that it may be easy to misunderstand and misinterpret the words as well as the actions of nineteenth-century immigrants.

After less than two years in America, the writer feels free to criticise the bishop of the diocese to which he used to belong without any sense of compromising his religious faith. On the contrary, it is both his religious faith and his worldly experience that give him the upper hand—and that allow him to begin his argument with a humorous yet serious pun. He has heard, he writes, of a rumor that life is not good in America. And so he responds: "That is true; I don't believe either that it is good here: could I not look forward to death, then it would not be good. But I thank our God and Father[11] who gave me the inclination to come here. You may live well here and sustain your life well." To paraphrase his argument: although the good life is something that awaits us after death, so that from this perspective life of course cannot be good in America, life here is nevertheless good in the strictly secular and temporal sense. Moreover—and this is the basis for his confidence in attacking the bishop—his decision to leave Norway and go to the United States was inspired by God.

When he then turns to polemics against the bishop, his strategy is to present himself as the one with actual knowledge and experi-ence of emigration and the United States while the bishop is charac-terized as one who "speaks of that of which he is ignorant." Thus the traditional relative status of clergy and common man, where it is the former who speaks with authority, is reversed. For even though the clergy may indeed speak from the pulpit against emigration, it is the uneducated and often lower-class emigrants themselves who have the real authority to speak on this subject. The present writer is not alone in reminding his readers that he knows what he is writing about while those who speak against emigration in Norway do so without any practical and personal experience. Indeed, he suggests that the bishop should limit himself to speaking about what should be his special responsibility: a concern for "people's souls." But, and this is where the writer goes beyond merely criticizing the bishop for speaking of that of which he is ignorant and becomes explicitly anti-clerical, the bishop is more interested in getting money from the peasants than in tending their souls. The bishop is against emigra-tion, the letter argues, because it threatens his income.

This leads to a point that is made in many an early immigrant letter and that is a criticism of an entire class rather than of the min-istry alone: the tendency among educated people to regard manual work as degrading. While the bishop keeps his hands soft and clean, using peasants to labor for him, "Here in America it is like this: all men work." And again as so often in these letters, the writer refers to his own experience as documentation. Indeed, in America there is mutual respect and love between employer and employee. Tellingly, it is an American clergyman who is used to show up his Norwegian counterpart in this regard. Lothe continues to refer to his own expe-rience which he contrasts with the bishop's lack of "understanding" and faulty information: "nor do I believe that he has ever seen it with his own eyes." Indeed, a man who can recommend "three cold val-leys" in the most northern county of Norway as an alternative to the twenty-four United States, can have no conception of the immensity of the writer's new country: "all of Norway is too small compared to any place in America."

In addition to experience Lothe also uses Scripture to counter the bishop's kind of "authority." Of course the bishop does not have it all wrong: "He does right in warning his brothers for the one road is long and dangerous." But he is wrong in claiming that God can only find those who stay in Norway, as he seems to suggest in his pamphlet. The one important thing is to "die with trust in God." Then it matters little how or where you die. So in taking leave with his brother and other readers of his letter, he adds the warning in Matthew 23 against "scribes and Pharisees," those who are "blind guides." Here Scripture is quoted as a parting jibe against the bishop of the Bergen diocese. Although later writers of immigrant letters do not commonly engage in polemics against the clergy, an expression of a religious sentiment at the end of a letter was a quite common way of giving closure to a message.

While we cannot draw any general conclusions about the religious sentiments of immigrants nor of the place of religious faith in their lives from a single letter, this reading does show that religious faith could be in harmony with anticlerical sentiments and that such a faith could be so natural a part of life that it entered into expressions of what we may think of as secular concerns. When talking about his health and his livelihood in Illinois and when arguing against the bishop, Svein Lothe demonstrates a theological bent. In this he may be special, but in my reading of immigrant letters of the mid-nineteenth century the expression of religious faith is more widespread than might be expected in correspondence where so many other concerns press for attention.

* * *

A relatively large number of the letters in the six selected years between 1847 and 1872 are letters concerned with the journey itself, either in reporting on the journey and the safe arrival or in giving practical advice on travel to those who were planning to follow. They are also packed with information of a practical nature about life under radically new conditions. Soil, harvests, building, income, and expenses were of crucial importance to both writers and readers. There are letters where religious faith is the central theme. In an assessment of the role and function of such faith in people's daily lives, the question of how religion enters into the practical spheres of life with which most letters are mainly concerned may be of greater interest.

In 1847 there are only five immigrant letters in *Fra Amerika til Norge,* and three of these refer to religion in ways that become quite standard for the genre in the following years.[12] One is the expression of religious sentiments at the opening and, more often, at the closing of a letter. This might be done at length and with obvious signs of much time spent with the standard religious literature of the day—as in this conclusion: "Could we all work while there is day and while the sun of grace may yet shine, so that we all could stand in readiness when the Bridegroom knocks on the door and wishes to enter, so that we then should be found worthy for the sake of Jesus and of grace be permitted to enter and become the Bride of Jesus and there celebrate the good wedding of eternity, so that we then could greet each other with faithful hands and with one heart praise God for the trials of the world and the priceless joys of eternity. Yes, may all of this truly happen; that is the wish of your faithful friend, Ole Stensen" (1, #21, 18 Feb 1847).[13]

More common is a brief acknowledgment of a shared faith, such as, "remaining for ever in God, our Savior . . ." (1, #24, 8 Nov 1847), or with words right out of the ritual language of the church service, such as, "God be with you!" (1, #23, 2 Apr 1847).[14] Just how much closing phrases of this kind speak of the place of religion in the lives of the letter writers may be a difficult question to answer. To me, however, it seems that the very fact that the words come so readily suggests that the religious views they express were to a large degree a natural and unquestioned part of their lives.

For some, such as Ole Stensen Karlsrud, it seems to have been a very large part. My co-editor of the first three volumes of *Fra Amerika til Norge,* Steinar Kjærheim, has observed that there seems to be a link between some of the immigrant letters in our collection and the many letters between Haugeans collected in the National Archives in Oslo. Indeed he sees the letter-writing tradition among Haugeans in Norway as a training ground for later writers of immigrant letters.[15] That Ole Stensen Karlsrud from Tinn in Telemark may well have had such a background is suggested by the pious conclusion I have quoted as well as by his opening, where he writes that the news, both good and bad, he has received from home may "in part serve as encouragement and edification and in part as abomination and fear and as a mirror, so that we might shun the old Adam and the destructive worldly imagination."[16] There are other similarly pious reflections in this letter, but what in particular relates it to Lothe's letter to Hardanger in 1838 is the way in which religion, political views, and agricultural concerns are expressed so that it is clear that they do not have separate compartments in the writer's life. After writing about the tribulations caused by the ague, he goes on to explain how good things may seem but for this death-bringing illness: "Had there been no adversities, then many would probably think: 'To be his own master.' Others would think: 'Here is the land of Canaan.' And yet others think and say: 'Here is Tabor, here we will build and live.'"[17] The two main advantages of the new land are political liberty and the fertile soil. The second is expressed in biblical terms and both the Bible-like phrases and the political sentiment are placed side by side as imagined statements by those who have shared the writer's experience.

Another manner in which the immigrants' religious concerns may be expressed is in the information sent home about congregational life and church matters. In 1847 immigrant congregations were limited to a few locations. The letter of 2 April is from one of these, Christiana in Dane county, Wisconsin, and the writer writes to his parents in Seljord in Telemark that "Pastor Dietrichson[18] has returned and this has brought joy to all who had joined his congregation," and adds that he taught school (that is, what was commonly called "religion school") in the southern district of the congregation while a man known all over that part of Telemark for his letters, Ole Knutsen Trovatten, taught in the northern one. Most of this letter consists of factual information on land, employment, and the prices of produce. The information on the congregation concludes a brief section on the statehood of Wisconsin, the war with Mexico, and taxes, suggesting that in this immigrant's mind, these were concerns of an equal status and importance.

There are sixteen immigrant letters from 1852. Of these all but four have some degree of religious expression. We may note that members of the educated middle class seem as reticent about their religion as most people in the secularized present. Two of the four letters without mention of religion are by such an immigrant, Elise Wærenskjold, in Texas.[19] Of the other two letters, one (#63) is entirely concerned with the settlement of the Norwegian property of the writer's deceased father, and the other (#71) is a detailed account of a voyage from Grimstad via Quebec to Muskego in eastern Wisconsin.

With a greater sampling of letters it becomes clear that pious phrases at the end of letters are indeed frequent but that they are in no way so standard that they appear to be clichés with little meaning.[20] Another feature that stands out is the tendency to relate expressions of faith with the major transitions of birth and death as well as with reports on health. Indeed, as we observed in the letter of 1838, immigrants tended to write about death as a transition rather than as a conclusion. "We know that time here is brief compared to the long eternity," as one writer in Norway, Racine County, Wisconsin, put it (1, #61, 19 Feb 1852). A natural and quite literal faith in an eternal life could be a comfort for people who knew they would not see family members again in this life, and it is often expressed, in a variety of ways. "Oh, may we see each other joyfully in the life eternal," writes Svend Larsen Haug as he is about to depart on a ship from Drammen (1, #66, 16 May 1852). One phrase that is found in several letters is that someone "has exchanged time for eternity" (1, #73, 15 Dec 1852).[21] The writer of this letter is just barely literate and her facile use of the phrase in writing to her immediate family about the death of her brother suggests that it was a natural way of thinking and speaking about death. Indeed, given the high rate of mortality among the early immigrants, death at an early age would seem more natural and certainly be more expected than it is in our more protected existence. This may be one way of trying to understand the matter-of-fact manner in which deaths of children are often reported in the letters.[22] This context may also help us to see why health and life could quite naturally be thought of as gifts of God and not to be taken for granted, a view that is expressed again and again as if health should not be mentioned except in gratitude.[23]

1852 is an important year in Norwegian-American church history. In January, 1851, the first meeting in the process leading to the formation of the Norwegian Synod in 1853 was held in Luther Valley, Wisconsin, and a second one in February, 1852, in Muskego. The process was controversial not least because of the fear many had of clerical dominance.[24] A few days after the Muskego meeting, Niels Hansen wrote a quite extensive report to his friend Jacob Abrahamson in Decorah.[25] The letter is an interesting document in that it illustrates how Norwegian lay piety also found a home in the Norwegian Synod. As Niels Hansen put it, "I wish my neighbors in Iowa had heard these deliberations. The Norwegian clergy are very much suspected by many and I must admit that I have not been entirely free [of such suspicions] myself. But by experiencing their basic principles at the synod [meetings] both last year and this year it has become clear [to me] that their views are correct. I wish that we could agree to have such a clergyman among us in Iowa" (1, #61, 19 Feb 1852).[26] When Svend Larsen Haug came to Elgin in Fayette County, Iowa, in 1852, his first impression of "the Norwegian clergy and schools" is also very positive and he writes approvingly of both Claus L. Clausen and Nils Olsen Brandt (1, #75, 28 Dec 1852).

Haug's letters are of special interest for a study of the role of religion in the lives of Norwegian immigrants since so many of the letters he wrote to his brother in Ål in Hallingdal for several decades are in the collection in the National Archives in Oslo. Here we may merely note that five years after his emigration, this Haugean, who at the outset was inclined to think positively of the "established" church and its servants, has become party to a conflict between those who "held to the truth according to the pure word of God," and a minister who "could not teach the words of Christ because he did not know the sound of his voice" and who "made the road to Heaven wider than the one Jesus has taught us." Now Haug relies on visitations by *Troende Præster* [ministers with faith], and first among these is Elling Eielsen (1, #135, 31 Mar 1857).[27] To follow Haug on his pilgrimage toward his "homeland" is far beyond the scope of this essay. We should note, however, that in their devout expressions of a shared Lutheran faith there is little to distinguish between Niels

Hansen, who found a haven in the Norwegian Synod, and Svend Larsen Haug, who was convinced that the Synod made "the road to Heaven wider than the one taught us by Jesus." Prior to emigration a variety of expressions of Lutheran piety had a home within the one established church, whether they were confessing Haugeans and so-called "readers"[28] or simply church-attending Christians who faithfully observed and received the sacraments. In Norway, too, members of a congregation could be concerned about the state of a pastor's faith and would welcome visiting lay preachers, but the notion of establishing a new congregation of the faithful and inviting a "believing pastor" from a competing church body was inconceivable to all but a select few in a society where people, social institutions, and church were one and indivisible. New attitudes and convictions about church organization were merely some of the many ideological, political, cultural, and purely practical changes in the lives of men and women brought about by immigration. By 1857 Svend Larsen Haug regarded a congregation as an exclusive group within a local community, not *as that local community.* Indeed, how could immigrants have retained the old-world system in a situation where the local community included people with other languages, cultures, and religious traditions? What separated Haug in Iowa and Hansen in Wisconsin in their initial choice of synod, then, may have been more a question of a difference in their responses to a new situation in a new land than of a difference in their Christian faith. One way of looking at the long process toward the formation of the Norwegian Lutheran Church of America in 1917 and, indeed, toward the formation of the Evangelical Lutheran Church in America in 1988, may be to see it as an acculturation process by which Norwegian immigrants became Lutheran Americans.

My reading of the other letters from 1857 as well as those from 1862 and 1867 confirms the impression made by the earlier ones. There are eighteen letters from 1857, and religion enters into the language of all but four, two of these being from the educated middle-class immigrant Frithjof Axel Meidell, whose descriptive and narrative abilities far surpass those of the other immigrant writers in the collection but whose communications with his family are entirely of a secular nature suggestive of a culture where religion has become not only a personal matter but a private one. Of the twenty-four letters from 1862, only fifteen express religious sentiments, but five of these are by Meidell and two others are from another family of a similar urban class and status. Of the twenty-two letters from 1867, only eight have no religious expression; one of these is from Elise Wærenskjold and another from the wealthy benefactor of the University of California at Berkeley, Peder Sæther.

A reading of these letters confirms that many of those traits observed in letters of the 1840s and 1850s were indeed characteristic of the way immigrants expressed themselves. Health is hardly mentioned without some expression of gratitude to God. Even if this may in some cases merely be a cliché, it is nevertheless an expression of a way of thinking and speaking that not only does not take health for granted but that quite naturally includes God—or at the very least the name of God—in nonreligious discourse:

> Both I and my parents, along with my siblings, all—thanks be to God—live well and enjoy health. (2, #70, 5 Jan 1862)
> We are, God be praised, all well and healthy as usual. . . . (2, #71, 14 Jan 1862)
> I am well and healthy and in all ways satisfied, for which God should be thanked. . . . (2, #72, 23 Jan 1862)
> It pleased us to learn that you all were well at that time and we may with pleasure report the same in return from all of us. God be thanked for his goodness toward us. He is one and the same. (2, #74, 22 Feb 1862)
> But we must nevertheless thank God that she died a peaceful death and was fully conscious until her soul departed. (2, #146, 26 Jan 1867)
> [We] are all well and healthy to this date, for which thanks should be given to the good God. (2, #147, 12 Mar 1867)
> And we see how our fortune may turn and therefore you must be happy that the Lord gives you health. (2, #148, 1 Apr 1867)[29]

A standard manner of expression surely reflects a standard manner of thought.

It is also characteristic of many letter writers to see their lives in time quite naturally under the perspective of eternity, as when "happiness and enjoyment in both time and in eternity" is wished for newlyweds (2, #74, 22 Feb 1862) and when "both bodily and spiritual" well-being is wished for an aunt and uncle "because we know that this frame is soon to be laid off" (2, #77, 5 Mar 1862).[30] Indeed, from this perspective there should be gratitude as well as joy regardless of the way things may appear here and now, as when one immigrant writes to his parents of his brother's death: "And we have received the same gift of grace [i.e., the good health reported in the letter from his parents] from our merciful God except that we have just experienced an adversity that seems both too big and too heavy to bear. But may God help us in our weakness. We should be as happy in adversity as in prosperity for He who wounds us He also heals us" (2, #89, 25 Jul 1862).[31]

There seems to have been no separate sphere for religion in the personal affairs of many immigrants. Nor is religion compartmentalized when they look beyond the personal and to the larger world of harvests, the economy, and politics. Immigration itself—as in the 1838 letter—is seen as ordained by God, as when a writer agrees that coming to America "is useful for all who do not have anything in Norway and who so desire. I believe that it is decided by God for all who believe that He is their benefactor, for man may plan his ways but the Lord prepares their path."[32] When writing of the Civil War (2, #71, 14 Jan 1862; 2, #76, 2 Mar 1862), of climate (2, #74, 22 Feb 1862), of finances (2, #79, 31 Mar 1862; 2, #147, 12 Mar 1867), and of harvests (2, #88, 16 Jun 1862; 2, #89, 25 Jul 1862) immigrants saw God at work.

As we may expect, ecclesiastical affairs are touched upon in many letters, some merely mentioning things that relate to congregational life, others also commenting upon theological differences. However, in my reading of this selection of letters it is difficult to see any significant theological or cultural differences in the religious expression of writers who may be identified with the synods that tended to hold up their differences as banners for their members. Indeed, where a synod identification is not made evident in a letter either explicitly or by implication (for instance by mentioning a minister's name) it would be hazardous to draw any conclusions from the quality or piety of religious expression. Juul Gulliksen Daaset writes from Fillmore County, Minnesota, that they are building a Lutheran church as well as a schoolhouse and that they have a minister, Nils Edward Schancke Jensen, who is both "kind" and "good." When he writes that there is much religious strife among Norwegian immigrants he specifies that "some are Franckeans and some are Methodists. Many places the husband goes to one minister and the wife to another so it seems that they have lost their senses. But," he explains, "most hold on to their old Lutheran church" (2, #72, 23 Jan 1862). Both this latter identification with the church in the old country and the name of the minister reveal that Daaset is a member of a Synod congregation, as does Johannes Olsen Nordhuglen's mention of the name [Ulrik Vilhelm] Koren (2, #74, 22 Feb 1862) and Ole Olsen Lie's of John Fjeld and Peder Marius Brodahl (2, #152, 29 May 1867), but there is little to distinguish them in their piety or religious expression from those who may be identified with the Haugean synod initiated by Elling Eielsen, such as Svend Larsen Haug (passim). Indeed, except for the latter, no writer in this selection engages in explicit theological controversy with another brand of Norwegian Lutheranism. It may be that the lines of demarcation were drawn more clearly in the decades to come, and that immigrants then became more conscious of belonging to one or another of the three main Norwegian Lutheran synods rather than simply to a local congregation. But my reading of the letters suggests that membership in a particular synod had not become part of most immigrants' identity in the early years. If further investigation should support this thesis there may be reason to consider the theological strife among Norwegian-American Lutherans in the nineteenth century as an aspect of their Americanization rather than as an aspect of their old-world heritage.

* * *

It is obviously true that the vast majority of the nineteenth-century immigrant letters that have been preserved for the most part "cry out about worldly matters," as the parents of an early immigrant from Tinn in Telemark complained in 1852.[33] This is hardly surprising given the novelty of their worldly experience as immigrants and their need to explain as much of this as possible to friends and family in Norway. The Christian faith they shared with their correspondents was certainly no novelty and this sense of a shared experience in spite of the separation and division of immigration may have been a motivation for some, such as Svend Larsen Haug from Ål in Hallingdal or Asbjørn Pedersen Mehus from Rennesøy in Ryfylke, to fill their letters with reflections on "the greatest and most precious good [which] is undeniably that we live in communion with God and His Holy Word."[34] As my preliminary investigation suggests, however, the immigrants who mainly wrote "about worldly matters" could not do so without revealing how, for them, the worldly and the spiritual, the secular and the holy, and, indeed, time and eternity were intimately and quite naturally connected. The secular attitude toward life dominant in later generations was in the immigrant correspondence of the mid-nineteenth century largely confined to the Norwegian educated and urban middle class, as exemplified here in the letters of Elise Wærenskjold and Frithjof Axel Meidell. This does not necessarily mean that for such writers religion was not a personal matter but that, in contrast with the manner of expression found in the majority of letters by members of the Norwegian rural classes, it was a private matter and not a natural part of their general discourse with family and friends.

This preliminary investigation has suggested two main areas in which a further investigation of religious expression in Norwegian immigrant letters may lead to a better understanding of the early foundations of a Norwegian-American immigrant culture and Norwegian-American institutions. The letters may help us to understand the nature of the Christian faith of the immigrant laity and its role in their everyday lives. They may also give us a better understanding of congregational life in the early immigrant churches and of the grassroots contribution to the emergence of different synodical organizations.

APPENDIX:

An Early Immigrant Letter
Translated and annotated by Orm Øverland

From Svein Knudsen Lothe
Chicago, Illinois, 10 July 1838
To Sjur Knudsen Aga, Ullensvang, Hordaland[35]

Dear brother, Sjur Knudsen Aga,

Time [now] allows me to report to you on my way of life. Right now I am in good health, but just after the previous letter I became ill and was in bed for several weeks and a doctor came every day for 3 weeks. And the doctor both thought and said that it would be the death of me, but I revived. My wife could not get out of bed for 6 weeks after her fever.[36] It was not so good for us according to the ways of the world but I hope and believe that it will be to our best. God the Father be praised and thanked who has upheld me long enough that I could learn to thank Him for it. I have a great desire to visit with you but an even greater desire to see you here in my home in Chicago. I hope to see you and your wife and children here.

The land is fertile everywhere on the prairies of Illinois. But all places are not equally good. In some places there is too much water. And the land is free for anyone to take and then pay for at 1 dollar an acre when it comes on the market.[37] This will not happen until from 3 to 10 years after you have taken the land. But there is also government land that you may pay for in cash. And there are wealthy buyers [who buy] much land and then sell it to others for 5 to 10 and to 15 dollars per acre. An acre is 12 1/3 rods, a rod is 5 yards, a yard is 1 1/2 *alen*.[38] Come to me my brother! Your children will thank you for it.

The most friendly greetings to all my siblings! Tell Ole Samsonsen Bleien and Willich Olsen Bleien that I would so like to speak with them; special greetings to Johannes Hovland, to Knud Olsen Børven and [his] brother Ole Olsen Espe. And then you must greet my wife's brother, Anders, and her mother, Durta, and her sister Gunnild that she must be ensured that she [i.e., the writer's wife] is in good health[39] and is satisfied and that she would be glad to have Anders with us.

You must believe that we live well. I have heard a rumor that it is not good here. That is true; I don't believe either that it is good here: could I not look forward to death, then it would not be good.[40] But I thank our God and Father[41] who gave me the inclination to come here. You may live well here and sustain your life well.

I know Neumann's thoughtful little book and have already read it.[42] But it is a good book that many praise, few read, and no one understands. But that he wrote: where is your pastor?[43] But I ask: where is his [unreadable word]? I believe that he speaks of that of which he is ignorant. Here there are such good schools where you don't pay a *skilling,* that his school where you have to pay money is not better.[44] But I also know what position he is in; he is in Christ's position and should speak well and tend to people's souls. I also believe that he is a clever bishop—for the fishing of money I believe he has an eye on each finger. Should his peasant slaves leave him, then he would himself acquire a peasant's hands and back [in order] to make money. Here in America it is like this: all men work. I worked for a pastor whose name was Uchalemo[45] and he worked just as well as I did. I know him and he knows me; he loves me and I love him, and that is our duty.[46]

In my daily fare I live as well as a wealthy man in Norway.[47] I would compare the bishop's intelligence to that of a flea. The flea will bite according to its understanding; and a man speaks according to his understanding; so they are alike. That is all I have to say on this matter. He who lay in the manger in the stall, He did not work for money. He would travel from one place to the other to find out those who desired to be cleansed. But He did not take on the authority of the beast in Revelation 13. You speak of the three cold valleys in the North of Norway[48] but that is far too little compared to the 24 United States of the good North America; all of Norway is too small compared to any place in America.

Neumann has written that Troy [N.Y.] sank.[49] That is a lie. I have traveled past this city and seen it. The bishop has never seen so beautiful a city in all his days, nor do I believe that he has ever seen it with his own eyes.—He does right in warning his brothers for the one road is long and dangerous. But it so happens that those die who do not come further than to the [local] church and who die at home; but I believe that it is the same whatever the manner of my death if I die with trust in God, whether I die at home and am buried in the churchyard with ringing bells or die at sea.[50] Take on the shield of faith and the helmet of salvation, which is the word of God; it is the whole armor of God that leads forward to life.[51]

I will conclude my letter with a loving and friendly greeting to all who ask about me. I have much to tell but do not have the time. Adieu. Live well! Be careful of blind guides (Matthew 23); woe to you who whitewash for the eye.[52]

Friendly greetings from your friend and brother,
Svend Knudsen

A note at the end of this copy reads: According to a copy sent from *lensmand* [sheriff] Age [Aga] to Bishop Neumann.[53] Attested by J. Storm.

NOTES

[1]This may be illustrated by Ingrid Semmingsen's *Norway to America: A History of the Migration,* trans. Einar Haugen (Minneapolis, 1978). Here the first 105 pages of the 172 in all are devoted to the forty-year period 1825-1865. The first quotation above is from David Monrad Schøyen, *Amerikas forenede Staters Historie. Anden Del: Unionen indtil Borgerkrigen* (Chicago, 1875), 407. The second is from a letter sent from Telemark to immigrants in Iowa, in Orm Øverland and Steinar Kjærheim, eds., *Fra Amerika til Norge,* 3 vols. (Oslo, 1992–1993), 1:220. The original reads: "Det er vist et stort Gode fra Forsynet, at han tilsender os saameget af dette Jordiske, at vi kunne leve med Lyst og Fryd; men det største og meest uskaetrelige Gode, er unægtelig det, at leve i Samfund med Gud og hans hellige Ord, og derpaa have vi den allerhygeligste Efterretning fra Eder. Vi høre vel og see mange Amerikabreve; men i de fleeste skriges der blodt over det Jordiske, og det som hører alene til dette

liv. Om dette, saavel som om hiint, have vi i Eders Brev en sandfærdig Beretning, vi takke Eder hjertelig for Brevet!" Translations are mine.

[2]Aspects of this interaction are the topic of my book, *Immigrant Minds, American Identities: Making the United States Home, 1870–1930* (Urbana and Chicago, 2000).

[3]Cultural rather than theological differences led Norwegians to leave the Swedish-dominated Augustana Synod in 1870. Two church bodies formed on the basis of the breakup of that synod (the Norwegian Augustana and the Norwegian-Danish Conference) and a group that left the Norwegian Synod in 1886 formed the United Norwegian Lutheran Church in 1890.

[4]It would be a grave error to pretend that all historians have been blind to the way in which religion has permeated all aspects of immigrant life. Øyvind Gulliksen has for instance shown how the language of religious expression and of immigrant experience are merged in standard discourse in the Hauge Synod. See his *Double Landscapes, Midwestern Texts: Studies in Norwegian-American Literature* (Ph.D. diss., University of Bergen, 1999). Victor Greene has shown how nationalist ideology and religious faith were inseparable in the development of the ethnic identities of Polish and Lithuanian immigrants in Chicago. See his *For God and Country: The Rise of Polish and Lithuanian Ethnic Consciousness in America 1860–1910* (Madison, WI, 1975).

[5]These two paragraphs paraphrase Orm Øverland, "Learning to Read Immigrant Letters: Reflections towards a Textual Theory," in *Norwegian-American Essays 1996*, ed. Øyvind T. Gulliksen et al. (Oslo, 1996), 223, 218–219.

[6]See Orm Øverland, "Innledning," in Øverland and Kjærheim, *Fra Amerika til Norge*, 1:36–38; and Øverland, "Learning to Read Immigrant Letters," 211–213.

[7]These and other questions are discussed in Øverland, "Learning to Read Immigrant Letters."

[8]Three volumes of *Fra Amerika til Norge* covering the period 1838–1874 were published in 1992 and 1993. Four more volumes of selected letters from the period 1875–1914 are projected.

[9]Øverland and Kjærheim, *Fra Amerika til Norge*, 1:41–43. An annotated translation of this letter is included as an appendix to this article.

All subsequent references to letters from the three volumes of *Fra Amerika til Norge* will be identified by volume, letter number, and date. This letter, then, as I, #1, 10 Jul 1838. The original for quotations from other letters will be given in the notes. There is at times some guesswork involved in reading these letters.

[10]Jacob Neumann, *Varselsord til de udvandringslystne bønder i Bergens Stift: Et hyrdebrev fra Stiftets Biskob* (Bergen, 1838). Trans. by Gunnar J. Malmin as "Bishop Jacob Neumann's Word of Admonition to the Peasants," *Studies and Records* I (Northfield, Minnesota, 1926), 95–109.

[11]A reason why it may at times be difficult to interpret passages in early immigrant letters is not only their handwriting but that the writers could have quite vague notions of grammar, syntax, spelling, and punctuation. It may be that the intended meaning here is not "our Father" but "our father," that is Knud Lothe, the father of the writer. While the letter, however, includes greetings to the writer's mother-in-law, there is no mention of the writer's parents, who may therefore be assumed to be dead.

[12]When I specify that the letters I discuss are "immigrant letters," this is because there are other letters relating to immigration that were actually written in Norway, either to immigrants or by prospective immigrants.

[13]"Kunde alle arbeide medens det er Dag og medens Naadens Sol skinner, saa at vi kunde staa rede, naar Brudgommen banker på og skulde komme ind til ham, at vi da maate værdes for jesus Skyld af Naade at gaae og komme derind og blive Jesu brud, og Drikke der Evighedens gode Bryllup, saa at vi da kunne hilses hverandre med trofaste Hænder og med eet Hjerte love Gud for den her i Tiden opstandne Strid, og det hisset i Evigheden for den uskatterlige Glæde—ja gid at dette alt sammen måtte således ske, ønskes af Eders fortolige ven, Ole Stensen." The text of this letter is as in the newspaper *Rjukan Dagblad*, 19 June 1937.

[14]"For blivende allthid i Gud vores Frelser"; "Gud være med eder!"

[15]Steinar Kjærheim, "Innledning," in Øverland and Kjærheim, *Fra Amerika til Norge*, 3:32.

[16]". . . I hvilke vi derav skulle kjende noget til Opmuntring og Opbyggelse, og noget til Avskye, Skræk, og et Speil, at vi kunne skye den gamle Adam Og Verdens grasserende Fantacie."

[17]"Skulde her ikke være noget imod, saa kunde nok Endeel tænke sig: 'at være sin egen Herre.' Endeel tænke sig: 'her er Canaans Land.' Atter Endeel tænke og sige: 'her er Tabor, her ville vi bygge og bo.'"

[18]J. W. C. Dietrichson immigrated in 1844 and established ten congregations in Wisconsin before returning to Norway in 1850.

[19]Another middle-class correspondent in these early years is Frithjof Axel Meidell, whose first letter is from 1854. His letters are also entirely secular in style and content.

[20]See *Fra Amerika til Norge*, 1, #60, 64, 66, 67, 68, 74, 75.

[21]"Har om skiftet tiden med Evigheden. . . ." Letters by this writer (Torgon Bjørnsdatter Tonga) and her siblings form the narrative in Orm Øverland, *"Det smærter mig meget at nedskrive disse Linjer til Eder": En utvandrerhistorie i brev* (Notodden, Norway, 1995).

[22]See Øverland, "Innledning," 30, and Øverland, "Learning to Read Immigrant Letters," 215-217.

[23]See *Fra Amerika til Norge*, 1, #60, 62, 64, 68, 76.

[24]See E. Clifford Nelson and Eugene L. Fevold, *The Lutheran Church Among Norwegian-Americans: A History of the Evangelical Lutheran Church*, 2 vols. (Minneapolis, 1960), 1:152-161; Orm Øverland, "Da embetsmannsklassen tok seg til rette i Vesterheimen," *Nytt norsk tidsskrift* 2 (1986), 49-61.

[25]There are several letters by Jacob Abrahamson in *Fra Amerika til Norge*. His son, Abraham Jacobson, became a minister. A descendant, Charlotte Jacobson, was for many years the archivist of the Norwegian-American Historical Association and the family farm is part of Vesterheim Museum in Decorah, Iowa.

[26]"Jeg sulde Ønsket at mine Naboer I Iowa Havde Hørt Disse for hanlinger. De Norske Præster ere meget Mistængte Af Mange, og jeg kan og saa tilstaa jeg ikke har været Aldeles Fri. Men Ved at ærfare Dems Grun Prinsipper saa væl det Faarige Aar som og saa i dette Aar paa Synoden, da er det klart at Dems Menig er og Rigtig. Jeg skulde ønske at vi kunde Blive Eenige om at faa en saa dan Præst i Jova i Blant os." Unavoidably, many of these writers may appear to be more literate in translation than in the original.

[27]The Synod pastor Haug has turned his back on is evidently Ulrik Vilhelm Koren, who had arrived in 1853 and served many congregations in this part of Iowa.

[28]Those who spent much time with their Bible and devotional books were called readers, *læsere,* often a synonym for Haugeans.

[29]"Baade jeg og mine Forældre, tillige mine Søskend leve alle—Gud ske tak vel, og nyde Helbreden." "Vi ere Gud være lovet alle friske og raske som sædvanlig. . . ." "Jeg er sun og frisk i alle maader vel Tilfres som er gud at takke for. . . ." "Da glæde det os at hørre at de var alle væl mæd Helsen den thide og det samme kan vi med god for nøielse beRætte tilbage i Jæn fra os alle samen. Gud være tak for sin godhet mod os. Han er den samme." "Men vei Maa aligevel Take gud for Hun Døde en Stille Død og Havde Sin gode Samling intil hun opgav Aanden." "[Vi] ere alle friske og vel til denne Tid, som vist er den gode Gud at takke for." "Og saa seer vi hvorledes Løkken kan dreie sig, og da maa dere vere glade at Herren giver dere Hilsen."

[30]". . . saa vel vi ønske Eder til Løkke i Eders Eægteskabes intrædelse og vi ønske Ededr baade glæde og god for nøielse baade for tiden og for Evigte." ". . . og Ønsker Eder alt Velgaaende, baade i legemlige og Andelige Henseender da vi veed at dette Pauluns Aflæggelse er snart forhaanden."

[31]"Og den same naadige gave har vi til dato imodtaget af vor naadige gud for untagen at det i dise dage har tiltaget os en modgang som synes for os at vere bade stor og tung at bere. Men gud jelpe os vi ere for svage. Vi burde vere ligesaa glade i modgang som medgang thi den som saarer han leger."

[32]"Det tror ieg Er Nøttige for alle som ikke har nogete i Norge og faar løste. Ieg tror at det Er bestemte af gud for alle [som] tror at Han Er deres for sorger, for menneskete optænker sin vei men Herren bereder deres gange."

[33]See the quotation from this letter that introduces this article. The quoted phrase below is also from this letter.

[34]There is a large collection of letters from Svend Larsen Haug in Riksarkivet in Oslo and many of these are included in *Fra Amerika til Norge,* beginning with volume 1, #66. Handwritten copies of letters from Asbjørn Pedersen Mehus to Morten Pedersen Nordhus are in Statsarkivet in Stavanger. They are included in *Fra Amerika til Norge,* beginning with volume 2, #16.

[35]The Norwegian text is a copy (with the superscript *Gjenpart* [copy]) now in the University Library of the University of Bergen. It is the first letter in *Fra Amerika til Norge,* 1:41–43.

The letter writer was from Kinsarvik in Hardanger and one of the eleven who emigrated from Ullensvang township in 1836, influenced by a letter from Gjert Hovland that is published in Theodore Blegen, ed., *Land of Their Choice: The Immigrants Write Home* (Minneapolis, 1955). This letter was brought to Hardanger by Elling Eielsen. Another member of the same group of emigrants was Sjur Jørgensen Haaeim who reacted unfavorably to his immigrant experience and wrote a negative account in a letter to Neumann that is also in the Blegen volume. An 1842 pamphlet by Haaeim is translated by Gunnar J. Malmin and published as "The Disillusions of an Immigrant: Sjur Jørgensen Haaeim's 'Information on Conditions in North America,'" in *Studies and Records* 3 (Northfield, Minnesota, 1928), 1–12.

[36]Literally, he writes that his wife "could not stand on the floor."

[37]This is a reference to the Pre-emption Act of 1830, a temporary law that was renewed several times and remained in force until 1842, giving squatters on public land the right to purchase as many as 160 acres at the minimum price of $1.25 an acre when the land was put up for sale or, as the letter has it, on the market. The preemption feature of this act was made permanent by the Distribution–Pre-emption Act of 1841.

[38]An *alen* was a Norwegian measurement that corresponds to 0.6277 meters or about two feet.

[39]Literally, we are told that she "lives well."

[40]That is, the good life is in the hereafter, not in this world.

[41]See note 11 above. In "Learning to Read Immigrant Letters: Reflections towards a Textual Theory," I discuss the special demands on readers of texts by intelligent yet often only marginally literate writers.

[42]See note 10 above.

[43]This is a response to a series of rhetorical questions in Neumann's pamphlet, one of which is: "And where is your pastor—the man who has expounded for you the Law of God, and admonished you in faith, hope, and charity?" (Malmin, "Bishop Jacob Neumann's Word of Admonition," 102). Neumann is warning that those who emigrate are withdrawing themselves from pastoral care.

[44]The letter writer calls this school literally a "money school."

[45]The name is probably spelled according to the writer's sense of pronunciation.

⁴⁶That is, no one is too good to work here and there are no class differences. Very many letters make similar observations.

⁴⁷This too is a point that is commonly made in letters for several decades.

⁴⁸On the basis of information he had received from the parish pastor (Fleischer) in Alta in Finnmark, the most northern county in Norway, Neumann recommended settlement in three valleys there as an alternative to emigration.

⁴⁹To illustrate that the United States is a dangerous country, Neumann uses some newspaper notices about accidents and negative immigrant experiences. The one about the disaster at Troy is from *Morgenbladet*. Neumann's reference, in Malmin, "Bishop Jacob Neumann's Word of Admonition," 107, is to *Morgenbladet* 64, 1837.

⁵⁰Towards the end of his pamphlet the bishop asks the peasants of his bishopric to reflect on how it would be to die in a strange country and asks, "when you are far away from all that has been dear to you, who shall close your eyes in the last hour of life? A stranger's hand! And who shall weep at your grave? Perhaps—no one!" (Malmin, "Bishop Jacob Neumann's Word of Admonition," 108-109).

⁵¹Phrases in this sentence are from Ephesians 6:10-16.

⁵²This phrase is not quite clear. In the compound *øienskalke* the first word is "eye" and the second is "whitewash" and the reference seems to be to Matthew 23:25-26. The meaning is to warn against a concern for appearances only.

⁵³This indicates that the sheriff considered the letter subversive and saw to it that the bishop had a copy. Since such letters were frequently both read aloud for friends and neighbors and copied and distributed, it is natural that the sheriff should get to know about it.

"Suffered under Pontius Pontoppidan" or "Good, Old Pontoppidan"?

Bjørn Sandvik

DURING THE BLOODY BATTLE of Murfreesboro at the end of 1862 and the beginning of 1863, one of Colonel Hans Christian Heg's Norwegian-American soldiers from the Fifteenth Wisconsin Regiment, Lars Dokken, lay wounded on the field. When he noticed southern soldiers approach, Dokken feigned death. He described his encounter with the enemy in minute detail in a letter to his relatives. "I was left lying on the field and the rebels swarmed around me from all directions. One of them swore and shouted, 'Here is a damned Yankee.' I lay still, but, of course, they had to take something from me, so they stole my blanket, my canteen, and a red leather wallet where I kept all the letters I had received from you. They also took a packet containing needles, thread, and such things. And, finally, they took the explanation of the catechism from me, which I regret the most."[1] Of all the things necessary to a soldier in battle, things that could only be carried in pockets and rucksack, what this lad least wanted to lose was his copy of Bishop Erik Pontoppidan's *Truth unto Godliness,* an explanation of Luther's *Small Catechism.* First published in 1738, *Truth unto Godliness,* or just the *Explanation,* as it was often called, had for more than a century been the text for the basic instruction of the young in both Norway and Norwegian America.[2] For generations it had provided a common vocabulary for the Christian faith and guidance for the Christian life. Through long use it had earned the sobriquet bestowed on it, *barnelærdommen,* "the children's doctrine."

Pontoppidan's *Explanation* was, indeed, one of the first two books printed for Norwegian immigrants in the United States. The first was an English version of Luther's *Small Catechism,* printed in New York in 1841. A year later Pontoppidan's *Truth unto Godliness* appeared in Norwegian. The man who saw to the printing of these books was the lay preacher from Voss who had immigrated to Illinois, Elling Eielsen. This strong and stubborn man walked from Illinois to New York to have these books printed. This early story illustrates as little else could how Luther's *Catechism* and the trusted commentary on it by Pontoppidan were from the very beginning foundational elements of Norwegian-American Lutheranism.[3]

A little more than seventy years later, two Norwegian-American church bodies, the Norwegian Synod and the United Norwegian Lutheran Church, negotiated an agreement resolving decades of controversy about the doctrine of election. Since the 1880s, polemicists had taken two positions in this strife. One the one side stood those defending the doctrine of the Norwegian and Missouri Synods. This was the so-called "first form" of the doctrine of election, which taught an unqualified understanding of predestination to salvation based on Article XI of the *Formula of Concord.* On the other side stood defenders of the position of the United Church, the "second form," which propounded a doctrine of election based on Question #548 of Pontoppidan's *Explanation.* In this famous question and answer Pontoppidan, in common with the Lutheran scholastics of the seventeenth century, set forth a doctrine of election which held that God elects people to salvation in view of divinely foreseen faith (*intuitu fidei*). The theological arcana of this controversy need not concern us further here. What is important for our purposes is that the union committees charged with resolving this protracted controversy eventually declared that both forms of the doctrine of election were acceptable. In the "Madison Agreement" of 1912 the committees declared: "The Union Committees of the Synod and the United Church, unanimously and without reservation, accept that doctrine of election which is set forth in Article XI of the *Formula of Concord,* the so-called First Form and Pontoppidan's *Truth unto Godliness,* question 548, the so-called Second Form of Doctrine."[4] In the matter of election, the colloquists thus gave Pontoppidan's text a status equivalent to that of one of the Lutheran confessions, the *Formula of Concord.* This statement was later approved by conventions of these two bodies as well as by the convention of Hauge's Synod and became a part of the basis on which the three bodies united to form the Norwegian Lutheran Church of America in 1917. As late as 1917, then, Pontoppidan's *Explanation* had unique authority among Norwegian-American Lutherans. One might say that the one and only way to church unity for Norwegian Lutherans in America was to organize them under both the Lutheran confessions *and* the old Norwegian doctrinal standard, Pontoppidan's *Explanation.*

Who was this Pontoppidan?

Confirmation was introduced into Denmark-Norway by decree of the pietistic King Christian VI on 13 January 1736. Two years later Erik Pontoppidan (1698–1764), then a pastor in Copenhagen and later Bishop of Bergen, published his *Explanation* for use in catechization in the churches and instruction in the schools.[5] The history of confirmation in Denmark-Norway is a long story, but from this time forward the authorities of the church oversaw the practice of confirmation in the realm.[6] As it was introduced in the eighteenth century, confirmation was constituted by a cycle of activities including instruction, catechization, official examination in the church, and the liturgical acts of confession and blessing. The new order of confirmation was, in fact, one of the most radical changes to occur in the life of the Church of Norway since the Reformation, and it was a long step toward the emergence of the modern Norwegian culture. Confirmation can rightly be called the mother of Christian instruction, widespread literacy, and the public school system in Norway. It was after the introduction of confirmation that *reading* first became a Christian virtue among Norwegians, and when the first revival movement took place under the leadership of Hans Nielsen Hauge (1771–1824), awakened folk were quickly called "readers" or *lesere.*

What were they reading? The Bible, of course, but the Bible societies had not yet been founded, and we know that the number of Bibles in circulation was very small. The readers more often read sermon books, the hymnbooks, and, of course, the *Explanation*. Bishop Per Juvkam, who is from Valdres, told me some time ago that even as late as sixty years ago old folks would tell about persons who were *gode til å lesa boki*—"clever at reading the book." *Boki*, "the book," to be sure, was not the Holy Bible, but the catechism.

Today it would scandalize us to hear of a book for children with 759 questions and answers to be memorized. It would comfort us but little to learn that in a later revision of 1762 by Peder Saxtorph (1730–1850), the number was reduced to only 451.[7] We have assumed that children had to learn all these questions and answers by heart. But did they really? Do we know how the catechism was actually used? What, in fact, do we know for certain about Christian instruction and confirmation as a whole in Norway in the eighteenth and nineteenth centuries?

My thesis is that our knowledge about catechization in this period is very limited, probably incorrect, and defined to a large extent by polemic and caricature. Professor Oddvar Johan Jensen of *Norsk Lærerakademiet* in Bergen has undertaken preliminary research in this field, and I will not discuss his findings in detail.[8] My intention here is rather to take the use of Pontoppidan as a short case study to demonstrate how *comparative, transatlantic* studies can yield new data and a better understanding of the Norwegian Lutheran churches in both Norway and the United States. In my own recent study of the decline in participation in Holy Communion in Norway, I have used American sources to mirror the development in Norway.[9] I use the Norwegian-American material as a *trollspeil*, a "trolls' mirror." Henrik Ibsen reminds us of the trolls' mirror in *Per Gynt*. The mirrors of the trolls are very special. When you look into such a mirror, you see yourself as the trolls do. The mirror distorts and creates odd images, but at the same time it accurately reflects the image of the person looking into it. In it, one suddenly sees oneself as others do. In the trolls' mirror, one sees as the trolls do; it is nevertheless a mirror, and one sees in it details and colors that are not easy to see in an ordinary mirror. I use this metaphor to describe the possibilities and limits of comparative study. Through comparative study, we attempt to see ourselves from the perspective of another who is like us, but also different from us. *"Vi ser likheten i forskjellene, og forskjellene i likheten,"* as Professor Bernt Oftestad of Menighetsfakultetet in Oslo likes to say. "We see similarity in the differences and differences in the similarity." The method must be used carefully, but I am nevertheless convinced that we on the other side of the Atlantic who are working on the history of the Church of Norway cannot neglect all the rich sources, written and unwritten, that can be found in America—*and only in America.*

"Suffered under Pontius Pontoppidan"?

If in the year 1912 one were to have asked someone in Norway about the status of Pontoppidan's *Explanation,* he or she might have recalled the old chestnut about the second article of the Apostles' Creed: *"født av jomfru Maria, pint under Pontius Pontoppidan"*—"born of the Virgin Mary, suffered under Pontius Pontoppidan."

The same person might also have mentioned the famous novel of Alexander Kielland (1846–1906), *Gift [Poison],* published in 1883.[10] This novel contains the most famous and brilliant caricature of Norwegian confirmation ever written. Dean Sparre, a conservative pastor and shepherd for the awakened, is known as an outstanding instructor of confirmands. Young boys and girls who have not been able to pass the confirmation examination and therefore cannot be granted the rights of adult citizens, including the right to marry, were sent to Pastor Sparre. He was reputed to be able to find small sparks of Christian knowledge even in the darkest and most hopeless minds. His secret weapon was a small black notebook, in which he wrote some mystical notes and numbers. One Osmund Asbjørnsen Sauemyren has tried to pass through the needle's eye of confirmation several times and now, at the age of nineteen, he is standing on the church floor for the examination. The poor lad had taken the *Explanation* with him when he worked as a shepherd on the meadows of High Jæren, and miraculously enough one answer has found its way into his limited intellect. Pastor Sparre has noted the number in his small black book. On confirmation day, as if randomly, he gives Question 503 to the poor boy.[11] The whole congregation is overwhelmed and impressed by the brilliant pedagogical genius of Dean Sparre as the young man quotes, by heart, the answer to the question about the means of grace. It begins: "This is the righteousness of Christ, the forgiveness of sins, the election of the children of God, God's fatherly care. . . ." This one of the longest answers in the whole book.

Kielland's novel is a brilliant piece of polemical literature. The question, however, is this: Has any ordinary confirmand in Norway or in America ever learned the answer to this question by heart? To my knowledge, no one has ever taken the effort to evaluate Kielland's attack in terms of its historical accuracy. Elsewhere in the novel Kielland writes that the boy Abraham, a lad from the Latin school, had learned the whole *Explanation* by heart. This might be possible for a clever student in a good school, but for the children of workers and peasants, who only had gone to the rather poor public schools of the era, this would most often have been impossible. As a matter of fact, Pontoppidan himself wrote in the preface to the original edition of the *Explanation* that about one-third of the questions were only to be read and not to be learned by young people without schooling. These questions are marked in his edition. Question 503 is, of course, one of them.

"Good, old Pontoppidan"?

Some years ago during a visit to the United States, I learned that there were many Norwegian-American Lutheran congregations named "Pontoppidan Church." My first reaction was: That cannot be true!

If we are to believe Alexander Kielland, the poor former confirmands, Osmund from Sauemyren and his mates, would never have dreamed of giving a congregation in the new world the name of the man under whom they had been made to suffer so cruelly. Yet according to the alphabetical index in the two-volume *Norske Lutherske Menigheter i Amerika 1843–1916*, at least ten churches named for Pontoppidan had been organized by the time these volumes appeared.[12] Looking at Norway in the American mirror, we suddenly see another image of this matter and discover something that prompts us to study the history of the Church of Norway more carefully. Upon closer examination there appear to be data to confirm that Pontoppidan was cherished in Norway as well as in America.

When a state commission published a slightly revised edition of Pontoppidan's *Explanation* in 1842, there occurred a conflict about the catechism that lasted more than two decades.[13] The opposition came from laypeople, from the leaders of the Haugean movement, and from ordinary folk in the parishes, all the people whom we have been led to suppose abhorred Pontoppidan. In some quarters opposition was certainly based primarily on theological considerations and reflected a considered opposition to the supposed Grundtvigianism of W. A. Wexels (1797–1866). On the popular level, however, opposition against the revised edition can also be seen as an expression of a spreading farmers' and peasants' revolt against the authorities of both state and church [*bøndeopprøret*]. It is as if the people of the church united to say: "This is our book. Do not touch it!" Pontoppidan had, in fact, written the people's book. Pastor J. J. Jansen notes in 1881 that an old farmer in Østfold asked him: "Is it true that the clergy will take Pontoppidan away from us?" "The clergy?" Jansen asked. "Yes, the teachers," the old man replied. And his final comment was: "Kick against it as hard as you can!"[14]

In 1867 a Norwegian pastor described the custom of catechization in the church in the summer months. The young people were to meet on certain summer Sundays the first two years after confirmation. The pastor gives us a vivid picture of what in contemporary terms we can only think of as a popular liturgical happening. He writes: "With all the young people, who appeared in large numbers and stood in long rows from the choir and down to the entrance, with the old folks watching with rapt attention, no living pastor could dream of using only the prescribed 30 minutes. In some places even the old people answer, eager to show that they still know their dear '*barnelærdom*.'"[15] This pastor had certainly studied theology, and it can be safely assumed that he had read the widely used manual of practical theology, *Collegium Pastorale*, written by none other than Pontoppidan himself in 1757.[16] Oddvar Johan Jensen has recently pointed out that in chapter 34 of *Collegium Pastorale*, Pontoppidan gives a description of his catechetical ideal and method that may today surprise those deceived by the myth fabricated so exquisitely by Kielland and others.[17] Pontoppidan's method is flexible and strikes contemporary readers as quite modern. He stresses how humor and a sympathetic understanding of the child's mental ability must guide the catechist. The instructor must, above all, not give the impression of being a *busemann* ["bogeyman"]. He warns against learning by heart without understanding. Jensen has had problems with convincing school experts today about these historical facts, about the *real* Pontoppidan, because we have forgotten how his methods and goals were changed and then attacked in the latter part of the nineteenth century. Lest we forget the trolls' mirror, it is also important to note that not only Pontoppidan's *Explanation*, but also his *Collegium Pastorale* were widely used during the era of the settlement in Norwegian America.[18]

Indeed, the term *barnelærdommen* appears over and over again in Norwegian-American sources as a *popular* term. In Norway as well as in the United States, Sundays in summer were popular among young people for many reasons.[19] First of all, they had a day off. The church was a social meeting place, where the girls and boys could mix. There was the chance for a flirtation or a fist-fight on the way home, perhaps even a drink behind the pastor's barn. In "Sætergjentens Søndag" by Jørgen Moe (1818–1882), for example, we hear the young shepherd girl up in the mountains sing her wonderful song. Watching the sun she sees that it is church time, and she is longing to go to church together with the others. She is dreaming of her boyfriend, of lifting her voice together with his. She is longing for Sunday social life down in the valley, where religious and social life are a unity, just as it should be according to the strong and healthy Lutheran doctrines of creation and salvation that relate the two sides of human existence.[20] We find the same sort of idyll in Norwegian-American sources from the Midwest, without the mountains, of course.[21]

Let us turn to some examples from America that shed light on the importance of Pontoppidan. One of the most striking comes from southeastern Minnesota. In the Christiania congregation in Goodhue County, Minnesota there was controversy as late as 1888 over the question whether the catechism and traditional sermon books should be recognized as *the Word of God.* Some were of the opinion that only the Bible could be called the Word of God, but for others the catechism also belonged in this category.[22] Another example of Pontoppidan's importance is included in a private letter from an old schoolteacher to Professor F. A. Schmidt in the days of the election controversy. "I have occupied myself with old Pontoppidan for so many years and days that I can not be moved to exchange the Lutheran doctrine with that of Calvin," the old man confesses.[23] It seems that both Norwegians and Norwegian Americans had already learned to sing: "Give me that old-time religion. It's good enough for me!" In this simple letter we find the key to interpreting the function of Pontoppidan's *Explanation* in Norway and America. This man has occupied himself with "old Pontoppidan" for "years and days." It was his curriculum for life. Naturally, one might say—since he was, after all, a teacher, and catechization was one of his principal duties. But Pontoppidan's *Explanation* was more than a schoolbook. It was a whole church program, a solid framework for congregational life, on the basis of which both layfolk and clergy were able to live and converse as Christians.

In my own work mentioned above I have tried to show how catechetical language dominated preaching, both in confessional and other sermons.[24] Pontoppidan provides a common point of reference for both pastor and congregation. In his essay in the present volume, Professor Orm Øverland of the University of Bergen has convincingly shown how the catechism and other popular religious texts gave the emigrants a shared language to express hopes and feelings in their letters to their relatives in Norway.

Norwegian-American Lutheran church life was founded on a trio of books: the very simple and informal liturgical order from *Kirkeritualet,* the Dano-Norwegian liturgical order of 1685; the hymnbooks that provided a common canon of hymnody; and the catechism. These books equipped Norwegians to sustain Christian life and faith in the United States on their own. The Roman Catholics, for example, needed a priest to celebrate a mass. Methodists required a discipline and what they called "the connection." The Norwegians, on the other hand, could gather in simple sod huts or houses for religious gatherings without clergy. They could provide for the instruction of their children in Christian faith and life from the reliable and time-tested *Explanation* by Pontoppidan. The majority of Norwegian-American Lutherans also retained the comparatively simple liturgical practices they brought from the homeland. Even when church life was more developed in later years, the majority probably did not exchange their old liturgy to conform to the more complicated military liturgical order based on Prussian ideals adopted in the homeland in 1889.[25] Most of them retained the egalitarian, participatory, simple liturgy brought to the United States by the first immigrants from Norway. Certainly in the hard early years, all they needed were the books, someone who could read a sermon, a person who could lead the singing, and a person to teach the children the catechism. Reader, precentor, and teacher were, in fact, often one and the same person. When pastors later appeared they were often expected to conform to simple practices already established. Scripture, hymnbook, and catechism had done their work well.

In both Norway and Norwegian America, church and school functioned as a unity during the period of the great immigration. Let us call it "the Pontoppidan pattern." Due to the primitive circumstances in the founding years, it is likely that they were not tempted to depart from the relaxed method of Pontoppidan himself. In examining the confirmation lists of a Norwegian-American congregation in the 1880s, one should not expect to find young girls and boys who can recite the 759 questions and answers by heart after six weeks of religion school in the summer or perhaps one day a week for "reading with the minister" during the winter months. It is hard to know what the occasional notation *særdeles godt* or *meget godt*— "exceptionally good" or "very good"—might have meant in those circumstances. On the other hand, one can expect to find young people who can read both Norwegian and English and who have studied the catechism in Norwegian. They know who they are; they are Norwegian

Americans and they are Lutherans. They know this because their congregation, perhaps one of the Pontoppidan churches, is a lively social and religious center where they have acquired a curriculum for faith and life from "old Pontoppidan" himself.

What can we learn about the Church of Norway by looking into the American trolls' mirror? "We see similarity in the differences and differences in the similarity." In Norway, we see modernity advancing on a rigid state church led by academically trained pastors during a very turbulent period. Most of the church leaders stood on the conservative side politically and they were regularly defeated on various issues. Politicians joined the conservative clergy in stopping the church reform movement, which had among other things sought the independence of the church from the state and self-governance for the congregations of the church. We see a new revival, led by Professor Gisle Johnson who sought to change the old Haugeanism and press it in the direction of German experiential theology, moving the center of theology from a concentration on the Word of God to a focus on the heart of the awakened believer. We find, as mentioned above, a new pedagogy and a new liturgy. None of this was very successful in defending the church against radical modernity or in assisting the church in adapting to a new context.

The first man who dared to criticize the Johnson movement was the Norwegian-American Professor Georg Sverdrup. He put his finger on the crucial point: the Johnsonians had no understanding of the congregation, he maintained, no ecclesiology. Sverdrup argued that Johnson was too strongly influenced by the individualism of Søren Kierkegaard, who, Sverdrup contended, had neglected the second of the two most important matters in Christianity, the congregation as the body of Christ.[26] Looking into the American trolls' mirror, we can see how radically church life in Norway changed in this era. In this crucial period in Norwegian history, the Church of Norway abandoned what I have called here "the Pontoppidan pattern."

The Norwegian-American church retained this pattern much longer. This is clearly illustrated in the remarks of Sverre Norborg in his introduction to an anthology of Norwegian-American Lutheran writings, *Fra det utflyttede Norge.*[27] It is noteworthy that Norborg had extensive pastoral experience in both Norway and the United States. He had, it seems, learned to use the trolls' mirror in both lands. Norborg notes that the first Norwegian-American congregations adopted Pontoppidan and Hauge as spiritual fathers and guides. This meant that these Norwegians remained "church Christians" [*kirkekristne*] rather than withdrawing from the church for the sake of purity of doctrine or to separate believers from unbelievers. Norborg further argues that the first emigrants sorely missed the presence of a pastor who could conduct the rites of baptism, confirmation, marriage, holy communion, and funerals. What were they to do about this? Longing for congregations, they organized them. Needing pastors, they ordained laypeople, although not often after the earliest years without giving them some theological training first. As Norborg saw it, neither rigid doctrinal orthodoxy in the style of the Missouri Synod nor an aggressive pietism determined to separate believers from unbelievers triumphed in Norwegian America. Both tendencies were ever present, but seemed to have appealed to some of their clerical leaders much more than they ever did to the members of the congregations. Norborg thus maintained that in the United States *"menigheten ble omtrent utelukkende folkekirkelig"* ["the congregation had almost entirely a folk church structure"]. Norborg is quick to note, however, that this expressed itself in a more pastoral and less authoritarian mode than in Norway. If slightly colored by Norborg's own national romanticism, his conclusion is nevertheless warranted: "The old Norwegian concept of the church [*kirkesyn*] won its victory in America."

Ironically enough, Norway abandoned its old concept of the church at precisely the same time it was adopted and adapted in America.[28] In Norway key leaders tried to guide the established church through the storms of modernity, but in many ways they failed. As a result the Lutheran church in Norway was divided between prayer house and official church; it was severely damaged by the importation of a new and alien German liturgy; and later on it was split by controversy over liberal theology. Most importantly, the bond between church and state remained intact. To this day Norway has a state church system, but sadly enough there is not a "Pontoppidan church" to be found. To find such a congregation one must journey to Norwegian America where congregations bearing the name of "Good, old Pontoppidan" continue to thrive to the present.

NOTES

[1]From Waldemar Ager, *Colonel Heg and His Boys: A Norwegian Regiment in the American Civil War,* trans. Della Kittleson Catuna and Clarence A. Clausen (Northfield, MN, 2000), 103.

[2]Erik Pontoppidan, *Sandhed til Gudfrygtighed,* was first published in Copenhagen in 1738. It has most recently appeared as *Sannhet til gudfryktighet: Forklaring over Martin Luthers lille katekisme* (Oslo, 1996).

[3]On this history see E. Clifford Nelson and Eugene L. Fevold, *The Lutheran Church among Norwegian-Americans: a History of the Evangelical Lutheran Church,* 2 vols. (Minneapolis, 1960), 1:77–78.

[4]This statement is from the so-called "Madison Agreement," or *Opgjør,* here as in an officially approved English translation in *The Union Documents of the Evangelical Lutheran Church with a Historical Survey of the Union Movement* (Minneapolis, 1948), 38–39.

[5]For Pontoppidan's life and work, Michael Neiiendam, *Erik Pontoppidan: Studier og Bidrag til Pietismens Historie,* 2 vols. (Copenhagen, 1933), remains the standard work.

[6]For the history of confirmation in Denmark-Norway, see *Konfirmasjon i Den norske Kirke gjennem 200 år, 1736–1936: festskrift til 200-årsjubileet, 13. Januar 1936, utgitt av Den norske Kirkes Presteforening* (Oslo, 1935); Brynjar Haraldsø, ed., *Konfirmasjonen i går og i dag: festskrift til 250-års jubileet, 13, january 1986* (Oslo, 1986) ; Brynjar Haraldsø, ed., *Kirke-skole-stat, 1739–1989* (Oslo, 1989). The *festskrift* of 1936 contains a chapter on Norwegian-American confirmation practice while the collection of 1986 does not.

[7]Peder Saxtorph, *Udtog af Pontoppidans Forklaring* (Copenhagen, 1771).

[8]See Oddvar Johan Jensen, "For 'døpte kristne' eller for 'udøpte hedninger'? Til debatten om Pontoppidans katekismeforklaring på 1800-tallet," *Tidsskrift for teologi og Kirke* 61 (1990), 21–34; "Etter Pontoppidan;

oppbrudd fra Pontoppidan, nye forklaringer, katekismen selv og en ny type lærebøker," in Haraldsø, *Konfirmasjon i går og i dag*, 185–199; "Fornyelse og kontinuitet; noen perspektiver på 444 års religiøs og moralsk oppdragelse i Norge," *Tidsskrift for kirke, religion, og samfunn* 4 (1991), 119–133; "Oppdragelse og undervisning i katekismens tid," in *Skolen, oppdragelsen, forbildene: foredrag fra Isegran-seminaret*, ed. Arne Bugge Amundsen (1993), 13–16; "Den pontoppidanske skolemester," in Haraldsø, *Kirke-skole-stat, 1739–1989*, 135–146.

[9]Bjørn Sandvik, *Det store nattverdfalle: en undersøkelse av avsperring og tilhørighet i norsk kirkeliv*, KIFO Perspektiv, no. 2 (Trondheim, 1988).

[10]Alexander Kielland, *Gift*, in *Samlede Verker*, 12 vols. (Oslo, 1949), 5:258ff.

[11]Numbering schemes have varied in different versions of Pontoppidan's catechism. In the original edition of 1738 this was Question 505. In *Sannhet til Gudfryktighet* (1996) this is Question 498. In this edition the passage reads: "Det gir oss Kristi rettferdighet, syndsforlatelse, fred med Gud, barnekår og dermed arverett til himmelen."

[12]See O. M. Norlie, *Norsk Lutherske Menigheter i Amerika, 1843–1916*, 2 vols. (Minneapolis, 1918).

[13]See Einar Molland, *Norges kirkehistorie i det 19. århundre*, 2 vols. (Oslo, 1979), 1:134–145.

[14]J. J. Jansen, *I stille Timer* (Kristiania, 1915), 115.

[15]"P-p." [pseud.], "Ogsaa om Altergangen i vore Landsmenigheder," *Luthersk Kirketidende* 9 (1867), 404. The term *barnelærdom* is not easily translated. "Children's doctrine," "basic knowledge from your child-hood," "elementary knowledge" are all far too pale and weak to bear all the rich connotations of the term in Norwegian.

[16]See Erik Pontoppidan, *Collegium pastorale practicum* (Copenhagen, 1757). This durable work has recently been published in a modern Norwegian version. See *Collegium pastorale practicum* (Oslo, 1986).

[17]Jensen, "Fornyelse og kontinuitet," 119.

[18]See Nelson and Fevold, *The Lutheran Church among Norwegian-Americans*, 1:106–107, 114–115.

[19]On the observance of Sunday in late-nineteenth-century and early-twentieth-century Norwegian culture, see Ann Helene Bolstad Skjelbred, *Søndag: Helg i Norge, 1870–1970* (Oslo, 1983).

[20]Jørgen Moe, "Sætergjentens Søndag," in *Samlede Skrifter,* 2 vols. (Kristiania, 1914), 1:38–39.

[21]For a description of an idyllic Sunday in Norwegian America, see Hjalmar Rued Holand, *De norske settlementers historie: En oversigt over den norske indvandring til og bebyggelse af Amerikas nordvesten fra Amerikas opdagelse til indianerkrigen i nordvesten* (Ephraim, WI, 1908), 137–141.

[22]The history of this congregation is included in Arvid Gerald Dyste, "The Causes of Religious Conflicts among the Immigrants in America: A Case Study of the Norwegian Lutherans in the Christiania Settlement in Minnesota from 1854–1904" (master's thesis, University of Minnesota, 1989).

[23]F. A. Schmidt papers, Archives of the Norwegian-American Historical Association at Saint Olaf College in Northfield, Minnesota.

[24]Sandvik, *Det store nattverdfallet.*

[25]The so-called "Short Form" of the Norwegian liturgy authorized for use in Norway in 1802 provided the basic pattern for worship in many Norwegian-American Lutheran congregations well into the twentieth century. For a sketch of this liturgy, see Nelson and Fevold, *The Lutheran Church among Norwegian-Americans,* 2:342–343.

[26]Georg Sverdrup, "Minder fra Norge," in *Skrifter i Udvalg,* ed. Andreas Helland, 6 vols. (Minneapolis, 1909–1911) 1:200.

[27]See Sverre Norborg, "Innledning," in *Fra det utflyttede Norge,* ed. Sverre Norborg (Oslo, 1930), 7–13. This is vol. 11 of *Hovedverker av den kristne litteratur fra kirkefedrene til nutiden,* 14 vols. (Oslo, 1929–1931).

[28]See Sandvik, *Det store nattverdfallet,* 158.

Marion John Nelson

Folk Art and Faith among
Norwegian Americans

Marion John Nelson

I CHOOSE THIS TITLE not only for its alliteration but also because
it poses questions that seek answers.[1] Can we, for example, rightly
speak of a Norwegian-American "folk art"? Very little in the artistic
activity of Norwegians in America can, indeed, be called folk art if
one applies the folklorist's traditional definition of that term. According to folklorists, folk art is a directly mediated tradition among
common people linked to a folk community. What there was of a
continuing folk art among Norwegian-American immigrants in fact
appears in the work of a few exceptional individuals and did not fill
any apparent need in the larger transplanted group. Individual creativity and impact from the new environment are generally stronger
in this art than any obviously inherited characteristics.

When traditional art was revived among Americans of Norwegian
background in the 1940s, it built on a lost and rediscovered tradition.
This made their art academic in origin and not at all the product of
direct transmission in the context of a folk community. This relearn-
ing, on the other hand, resulted in an art much closer to that of the
old tradition than are the few early examples of art from the earliest
Norwegian-American immigrant communities. The art of the later
revival tended to rely so directly on the past, in fact, that the elements
of intuition and spontaneity necessary to any living art tradition were
stifled. This art, however, found a base in the community, often being

perpetuated in local classes or study groups and even finding a market within the group. It had, from a socioeconomic standpoint, much in common with the tradition it emulated, but the art of the revival differed in having been relearned and also in the nature of the group in which it existed. The Norwegian-American artists of this era do not represent a clearly defined element in the total society as "the common folk" did in nineteenth-century Norway. These later artists rather constituted a mixture of many social classes and, to some extent, of various ethnic backgrounds. Their community resulted from living near each other, from simple proximity, primarily in Midwestern towns of strongly Norwegian background.

Equally as problematic as the term "folk art" is the term "faith." How can faith be depicted? Our criteria for its presence will be the use of images or texts associated with Christianity in its Lutheran form. Lutheranism was the official religion of Norway and, by the nineteenth century, it had also become the defining or at least a major element in the folk faith of Norway. Use of these symbols does not, however, guarantee presence of faith, the personal commitment to a power outside the earthly realm. As interpreters we must generally assume that the uses of these images or texts is evidence of such faith, while at the same time we must acknowledge that we may be incorrect in making this assumption.

The lack of a direct transfer of the tradition of folk art from Norway is not strange. The socioeconomic circumstances out of which that art had grown were rapidly disappearing even before mass emigration began in the mid-nineteenth century. The arts had no firm springboard from which to make the leap over the Atlantic. The self-sufficient economy and closed cultural units that were an important part of the context supporting folk art in Norway never existed or were short-lived in the United States. Such folk art as remains is the product not of sustaining communities but of a few personally motivated individuals.

The question of motivation in the arts is problematic because art falls outside the category of the rational. What motivates art? One can postulate special drives in human beings to imitate nature or to create forms with lines, colors, or masses with no specific prototypes in the visual world. These might be called "aesthetic drives" or, more appropriately, "art drives." This would make art a self-perpetuating category of human activity. Such thinking is not, however, much in favor today.

The close relationship between art and religion has been pondered ever since these two areas of culture first came under historical and philosophical investigation in the late eighteenth century. Especially during the past seventy-five years there has been increasing interest in the study of primitive cultures, in which art is the major source for documentation of religion. The most extreme conclusion on the subject is that of Ananda Coomaraswamy who, in *The Transformation of Nature in Art* published in 1934, argued that art and religion are not merely related but identical.[2] This has often been considered hyperbolic, but it cannot merely be dismissed. A balanced and lucid recent presentation is Earle Coleman's *Creativity and Spirituality: Bonds between Art and Religion*.[3]

Some of these ideas may help to explain why art appears without apparent rational explanation in isolated places, for example, as nonprofessional activity among individuals in pioneer Norwegian-American immigrant communities. Much in this art indicates that an affirmation of faith was an important part of its genesis. Cut off from the historical community that had nurtured their faith, the Church of Norway, and left with only unstable remnants of that church contentiously trying to find themselves as Norwegian-American denominations, certain individuals felt the need of making public statements, as clear as pictures and texts generally are, of their personal relationship to or understanding of the higher powers.

This, of course, is not unique to Norwegian Americans, and there is nothing new about considering the role of religion in American folk art. C. Kurt Dewhurst together with Betty MacDowell and Marsha MacDowell made an astonishingly comprehensive study of the subject in connection with the exhibition and catalogue *Religious Folk Art in America: Reflections of Faith,* in 1983.[4] It includes two of the works that will be studied here. While not commenting directly on the overwhelming role of religion in American folk art, this book and the related exhibition are certainly evidence of connections between folk art and faith. This is not surprising, considering that many of the early settlers, including some Puritans and parties of Pennsylvania Dutch, were members of religious societies that emigrated as groups. Spanish immigrants, to take another example, came from a society that was very much defined by the faith and life of the Roman Catholic Church. The dominating role of faith in the American environment into which the Norwegian immigrants came may thus have meant as much for the role of religion in their few and isolated examples of early artistic creation as did any direct inheritance of the religious folk art of Norway. Religion does not, in fact, have a prominent place in Norwegian folk art, although a few individual artists like the woodcarver Iver Gunderson Øvstrud (1711–1795) used almost exclusively religious subject matter. Even with these artists, however, it is difficult to know whether the appeal was religious or simply the result of an attraction to the human figure. Bible illustrations were certainly the most accessible if not the only models for such figures.

Prestige and social identity rather than faith seem to be the major concerns in most Norwegian folk art after 1700. This is certainly true of the decoration on dowry chests and drinking vessels. It is largely the case with room decoration as well, although powerful uses of religious images do appear in the painted interiors of Ola Hansson (1761–1847) in Telemark and in the work of Herbrann Sata (1753–1830) and his sons in Hallingdal. Longer inscriptions are often from the Bible, but shorter sayings of the kind that appear on ale bowls are more often secular.

Untrained immigrant folk artists

Coming to America from Sogndal in 1864 with training in carpentry and blacksmithing, Lars Christenson (1839–1910) did not bring a well-developed artistic vocabulary with him. As the son of a schoolteacher, on the other hand, he was literate and undoubtedly well versed in the Bible and in devotional texts. It was probably his familiarity with these writings that led to his detailed observation of at least one typical seventeenth-century altar of professional production and supported his capacity to retain an image of it, even to its details, in his memory for over thirty years.

The first known work of Christenson after he settled near Benson, Minnesota in 1866 is a mammoth two-piece cupboard with drawers and a high enclosed cabinet at the top. It likely cannot be dated before the 1880s and certainly was made as a practical piece for his home. The simple decoration of this piece, however, indicates that Christenson already associated his art with his Christian faith. The crown of the mirrored scrolls is outlined by two serpents whose tails form a double spiral at the top and whose bodies follow the curvature of the scrolls down to the heads at the bottom. The serpents have apples in their mouths and they offer their tempting fruit in opposite directions. There is no Eve to receive them. The observer is the person tempted. The serpents serve as reminders to those who see them of temptation's constant presence. The artist's son told me close to fifty years ago that this was his father's interpretation of the motif and that these images were put there as a lesson to the children. This makes the work not only an affirmation of faith. It also includes the didactic element so often found in religious folk art.

Although the religious message behind the image of the tempter was undoubtedly the major motivation for this carving, Christenson may, as we will also see later, have carried images in his memory that helped him arrive at the form he chose for this piece. He was baptized, confirmed, and married in the old Stedje stave church, which was dismantled three years after he emigrated. Its portals are in the Bergen Museum and have the writhing serpentine dragons characteristic of twelfth-century stave church portal decoration. How do they relate to Christenson's tempters? Not ordinary serpents, these creatures have the two front feet characteristic of stave church dragons. Such dragons never have apples in their mouths, but later folk art versions occasionally do. An example in Telemark, from possibly as early as the sixteenth century, is found in the Bergen Museum. Here snakes form the handles, also offering apples in opposite directions. A slightly different example from Hardanger is dated from 1845, when Christenson was six years old. It is now located at the private museum Little Norway, Mount Horeb, Wisconsin. This clearly indicates that the serpent with the apple was an element of the folk tradition in Christenson's native western Norway. The Christenson cupboard may be the only Norwegian-American work in which omens of pagan symbolism can be seen still lurking behind expressions of the Christian faith.

Lars Christenson's better-known altar clearly affirms and teaches the Christian faith (Fig. 1). In his altar he moved the Last Supper from its traditional position in the predella under the main panel to a place above it so that the picture of the meal could relate more clearly to the admonition expressed in the main inscription: *Dog Se, hans Haand som Mig Foraader er over Bordet med Mig* [Behold the hand of him who betrays me is with me on the table].[5]

Christenson seems to have made this altar not so much to fill a need in the local church as to make a statement of his faith and to warn against the danger of becoming a traitor to that faith. Lack of interest on the part of the local congregation is said to have contributed to the altar's never having gotten its intended position, but the artist's declining health may also have played a part. He took the altar to the Minnesota State Fair in 1904, with the three lower panels yet to be carved, and essentially abandoned it in St. Paul. When it was taken out of the warehouse where it had been stored in 1910, the year of the artist's death, it went to the Luther College Museum (now Vesterheim) in Decorah, Iowa, rather than back to Benson. Whether this was carrying out the wish of the artist or a wise move on the part of college president C. K. Preus, who claimed it for the museum, is not known. The shift may have been fortuitous, because in its place in the central museum of the Norwegian Americans it has received attention that it may not have gotten in a remote parish church.

Lars Christenson's altar is a well-conceived totality created by an artist firm in his faith but limited in his models for expressing it. The primary message is salvation through Jesus Christ. The secondary message is the ease with which that salvation can be betrayed. The overall plan is that of the German Baroque altars found throughout western Norway as a result of the presence of Hanseatic merchants who retained a stronghold in the area during the early seventeenth century. The altar from Orskog Church in Sunnmøre has not only the three-part division both horizontally and vertically and the central position of the crucifixion, last supper, and ascension found in Christenson's work, but also several details hard to explain from other sources. It is now in the Bergen Museum. If it was acquired by the museum before Christenson spent the year 1863 in that city, he would have had an opportunity to study it in detail. Museum records are unfortunately not completely clear on this issue. Features the two altars share include cherub heads and wings surrounded by scrolling vines, caryatid figures at the bases of the posts, and heads in the middle of the posts. While only two of the caryatids and heads appear on the Orskog altar, four are found on that of Christenson. He identified the former as the major prophets on which the gospel rests and the latter as evangelists who saw and recorded episodes from the life of Christ.

The caryatids on the Orskog altar are actually angels carved in low relief against the rounded bases of two posts, and the heads are grotesque masks that were commonly a part of Baroque decorative tradition. Christenson had to bring these into a coherent theological scheme. When, in the early 1960s, I asked Christenson's son about his father's working methods, Hans Christenson said that his father just looked in the Bible and carved. Hans Christenson assumed that his father was using the Bible for divine inspiration, but all seven panels that Christenson completed had obvious models in a special edition of the Bible published for Norwegian Americans by the Waverly Publishing Company in 1890.[6] Christenson certainly gained more than divine inspiration from his study of the Bible. He also found models for his work there.

Christenson brought his own artistic vision to the academic illustrations drawn largely from nineteenth-century sources. Stylistically they were reduced to reliefs on a flat ground with little linear perspective. Six were vertical in orientation and had to be made horizontal or square to fit the overall design of the altar. These problems were handled with masterful imagination, giving a consistent decorative quality to the altar's surface.

The liberties that Christenson took with his models were not only dictated by design and technique but also by the nature of his message. His theme is obviously redemption through the crucified Christ. Christ is the dominant image, and Christenson makes Christ's head the centerpoint, the focus of the entire composition. It is also the largest single image in the altar, with the scale of what surrounds it gradually diminishing until the heads of the figures in a peripheral circle are less than one-fourth the size of Christ's. Although the expressive and decorative quality of the carving keeps improving from that in the two upper panels, which are known to have been carved first, down to the nativity, which appears to have been last, this quality is at its very finest in the head of Christ. The earthly suffering here has been transformed to convey perfect peace and spiritual victory.

In his altar Lars Christenson created a work in which few could deny that art and religion have been brought into perfect unity. No other immigrant artist ever achieved this to the same degree. Perhaps the closest parallel is to be found in the work of his slightly younger contemporary, John Rein (1858–1916). Rein's best-known work is an altar painting of the Last Supper from 1895 for the Rose Church near Roseau in northern Minnesota (Fig. 2). This painting was part of a large commission for a church building and furnishings for the congregation. It is, however, difficult to determine to what extent the altar was the product of Rein's personal faith. It could have been merely one item from the congregation's specifications. This seems unlikely, not only because of the special attention he appears to have given it, but because by 1895 professional altar painters were regularly available and builders had generally ceased to accept commissions for altar paintings. The altar painting was apparently an assignment Rein himself wanted. It is one of the most original and inspired altar paintings by a Norwegian-American artist. The professional altar painters produced almost exclusively copies of known works, but here the folk artist John Rein has created an original work.

Rein's point of departure in painting his altarpiece, like Christenson's, must have been the memory of one or more works he had seen before he emigrated. The Last Supper was not a common altar subject in Norwegian America, but it appeared frequently as the central image of altars of the seventeenth and eighteenth centuries in Norway. In these paintings, the disciples surround or partly surround the table, which often has a chandelier hanging above it. This is the type Rein created. For the portraits of the individual disciples he needed help that remembered images could not supply. Like Christenson, Rein turned to an edition of the Holman Bible that included a gallery of portraits of the apostles based on Leonardo. The relationship of St. Thaddeus in this gallery to that in Rein's painting is especially close.

Rein's altar, like that of Christenson, is a textbook example of how remembered Norwegian images have merged with immediately available American models to arrive at a pictorial form for the affirmation of faith. That faith itself must also have seemed suspended between two worlds, since even the language in which it was conveyed was in transition. Lars Christenson uses Norwegian for all of his many inscriptions, except a translation of *En engel blant Blomster* [An angel among flowers], which appears opposite the original under a repetition of the same motif. Pictorial art must, indeed, have had special significance in the affirmation of faith for people caught between two languages. Images could relate equally well to both languages.

More direct evidence of Rein's personal faith is a very individual crucifixion scene on a window shade, apparently intended for his home. John with Salome and the mother of Jesus are shown just as they are departing from the barren and lonely Golgotha, while Magdalene still clings to the foot of the cross. It is evening with just a band of light remaining over the distant city. The very distinctive treatment of the subject indicates that it may not have had a Norwegian model. If there is an American prototype it has not come to light. In this work Rein has given us a mood painting of the lowest moment in the gospel story. The heralded Messiah is dead and no sign has yet been given of the great reversal to come. The uncertain execution of the figures reveals that Rein is a true primitive, but their simplicity, dignity, and a total lack of mannerism make this modest creation a moving work of art. Its success depends not on the facility of the painter but on the sincerity of the faith that motivated him. Faith was here functioning, as true faith may always do, as a facilitator of art.

What has been said about Rein's crucifixion also applies to the thirty-two biblical figures found on four doors painted by Martin Olson (1828–1881) at Elkhorn, Wisconsin, about 1860 (Fig. 3). They are unusual creations from the first decade in which artistic activity is known among immigrants from Norway. Olson could not have had much experience with decorative painting in his native Telemark before emigration, because his work reveals nothing of the distinctive decorative style of that area. He must simply have had a strong desire to give his religious faith pictorial expression. The doors were in the house of Americans with whom he was staying, and he found his models for the figures in a volume owned by them, *The Complete English Bible*.[7] All that he appears to have brought to his work from Norway is the idea of figurative decoration on doors and the use of Norwegian "*Cap.*" as the abbreviation for the English word "Chapter" in citing Scripture.

An example of the Bible that is said to have given Olson his models is located in the Webster House, Elkhorn, Wisconsin, although I have not had an opportunity to investigate it. Olson's figures, however, cannot be rote copies. The originals were undoubtedly in black and white, and Olson has rendered them in interesting and pleasing colors, said to have been prepared by him from natural materials. It is also hard to believe that the originals could have had the individual, expressive character of Olson's figures. Solomon is presented with the simple grandeur of the wise king, while Jonah appears with the exaggerated gesture and fanatic eyes appropriate to this more colorful prophet. Olson appears to have established a personal relationship with every figure in his Judeo-Christian pantheon. He was also painting for Americans in an American house. His models were not Norwegian nor is there anything clearly Norwegian detectable in his style. The most important inheritance from Norway in the doors is the deep religious faith that led him to his subject and gave his interpretation the inspired character of genuine art.

By way of contrast, we may consider the work of Peter Oliver Foss (1865–1932). Much of the unique art by this self-trained Norwegian-American artist of the Boston area is on biblical themes, but one feels that fascination for the exotic and dramatic subject matter rather

Figure 1. Altar. Lars Christenson.

Figure 2. Altar painting. John Rein.

Figure 3. Door. Martin Olson.

Figure 4. Painting: Samson and Delilah. *Martin Oliver Foss.*

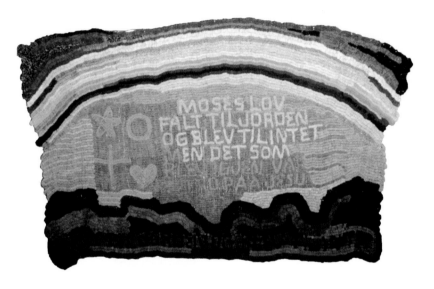

Figure 5. Pictorial textile. Nettie Halvorson.

Figure 6. Log chair (kubbestol).
Halvor Landsverk.

Figure 7. Wood carving:
Christ with Sheep.
Halvor Landsverk.

rty years ago, confirmed this. He said his mother neglected
usework and the children for about two years and devoted
ntirely to this piece.

e the individual symbols in Halvorson's tapestry are strong
r—a rainbow, a cross, a star, a heart, a circle, and rocky
-their combination may have been determined by things in
n's life and thought that we may never be able to fathom. It
hat the relation of law and faith had been at the center of a
problem for her. In faith she also finds hope, as indicated
verarching rainbow and the star; love, as indicated by the
d eternal life, as indicated by the circle. A ring, of course,
stand for unity and could relate to her marriage, but this
likely considering the high theological level of everything
e composition.

making of her statement appears to have been an end in it-
Nettie Halvorson. The piece is almost impossible to hang
e is no indication of her doing it for her church, where it
ve served as a rug within the altar rail. According to her son,
completed her tapestry she folded it up and put it in a
ere it remained until an auction was held on the farm years
death. Here is a work of art that makes a direct profession
without consideration for the earthly recognition that is
underlying motive in artistic creation.

e 1950s most art by ordinary people in Norwegian-American
ties represented an attempt to revive the old folk arts of
ut a few individuals continued to create more directly out
pulses within them, often to affirm their faith. Only two,
and a sister, Halvor Landsverk (1909–1998) and Margit
Mindrum (1899–1975), will be mentioned here. Their fa-
jel Landsverk (1859–1945), who emigrated from Seljord,
in 1884 to Whalan in southeastern Minnesota, had been
the revival of the old folk arts in Norway and became one
iest artists consciously concerned with reestablishing Nor-
rving on this side of the Atlantic. His major accomplish-
to revive interest in the *kubbestol* [log chair]. He produced
ately a dozen examples, some elaborately carved. Halvor

Figure 8. Painted wood plate. Norma Getting.

than his own personal faith may have
Here one faces the most critical proble
flection of faith. Faith itself has no tan
therefore lies outside representation a
discourse. One can identify it only thr
sociated with it, the most obvious b
from the biblical narrative upon whic

While Foss leaves us in a quandar
faith in his paintings, the textile artis
eth century) of Houston, Minnesota
with words and symbols that allow
known work by her is the so-called "N
years of the twentieth century (Fig.
brought to it out of her heritage is
some Christian symbols. The rest is
and imagination. This means that it
exceptional creation of someone with
The motivation must have been to n
in translation reads, "The law of Mos
nothing, but what remained was fai
6 1/2' x 11' surface, and the "fell to th
repeated along the lower edge. She d
an established medium but creates
with approximately 1" x 1" openings
warp. Packs of about twenty little pa
each square on one of the threads fo
sen for these patches make up the de
is created at the same time that the p
makes execution exceedingly diffic
amount of text. One must speculate
that she tried to follow or simply had
head that she could progress inch b
other example of work in this tech
carpet warp in hand, she arrived at a
she wanted to make. This seems to
sion, apparently a religious one. Halv

about fo
both ho
herself e
Whil
and clea
ground—
Halvorso
may be t
personal
by the o
heart; ar
can also
seems ur
else in th
The
self for N
and there
could hav
after she
closet wh
after her
of faith
often an
By th
commun
Norway,
of the im
a brother
Landsver
ther Tark
Telemark
exposed t
of the ear
wegian ca
ment was
approxim

Figure 9. Painted wood plate. JoSonja Jansen.

Landsverk followed in his father's footsteps, and by the time of his death in 1998 had carved about 330 traditional Norwegian log chairs (Fig. 6). While demand kept him carving *kubbestoler* to his very last days, his personal inclinations during his final years moved away from romantic Norwegian material to the image of Christ. A personalized version of the Leonardo Last Supper and images of Christ as good shepherd and with the children are his major late works, all in churches in his area. The most hauntingly spiritual of his late works is a free-standing figure of Christ with the sheep, carved by feel when he was virtually blind (Fig. 7). The accuracy of his sheep, which he as a farmer literally knew from feel, is impressive. The mystery in the head of Christ, which he left blind like himself and like the Romanesque Christs from the Middle Ages, is uncanny. Spiritual vision comes from beyond the human eye.

Nothing of Norwegian romanticism is found in Margit Landsverk Mindrum's work. Throughout her life she carried out the duties of housewife, which allowed little time for producing art other than rugs or other household textiles until she was fifty. She then turned to painting and produced about 600 works before her death at the age of seventy-five. Faith as a motivating force in Mindrum's work may not be immediately evident because her joy was in depicting her immediate natural environment in all the variations brought to it by changing seasons and weather conditions. But her letters and simple autobiography, *No Change My Heart Shall Fear,* as well as the character of her painting, indicate that her natural environment was also a spiritual environment in which God was always present.[8] She did not paint God. That, in a way, would have been redundant, but a meadow with sheep will often carry the inscription "The Lord is my Shepherd" or a rolling landscape will have the legend, "I will lift mine eyes unto the hills."[9]

Mindrum was a naive artist only in having no academic training other than some counsel from her brother, who knew the fundamentals of representation from taking a correspondence course in art. That she was untutored, however, did not keep her from developing her own medium. This was "Carter's Water Colors," a kind of gouache often generically referred to as "poster paints," available at local dime stores. To develop this simple medium, she blended the commercially available colors as if they were oils and gave the landscapes the most subtle of shading. Her painting never has the flat and linear quality expected in a self-trained artist. Her need for expressing the beauty around her, which was one with that of God, was so great that she brought herself in short order to the level of an academic realist.

THE REVIVAL OF FOLK ART IN NORWEGIAN AMERICA

A nostalgic desire among the immigrants to link themselves with the culture of their ancestors has often been thought of as the primary motivation for the revival of traditional Norwegian folk art in America. In Norway it is still looked on that way and is not taken seriously as artistic expression. The vitality and creativity in much Norwegian-American folk art makes it difficult for me to accept it as the product of so weak an emotion as nostalgia. A need for identity in the impersonal environment of America seems a more likely explanation. Even this, however, is not completely adequate, because of the tendency for the revival to spread among people of other ethnic backgrounds. Half the blood in the veins of one family of American painters working in the decorative style of *rosemaling* [rose painting] that I studied several years ago proved not to have been Norwegian at all. My conclusion for some time has been that the revival resulted from a frustrated desire among immigrants, women in particular, for artistic expression, and that this was met by the discovery in the 1930s of a forgotten tradition in their own ethnic background. The frustration was something shared by the entire community, and when Norwegians came up with a solution, artists of other ethnic backgrounds were ready to share it with them.

Only recently has it become evident to me that a desire to express personal faith may also have played a role in the revival. This is especially evident in weaving, where much of the energy of the revival has moved toward the creation of vestments and paraments. This, in turn, led to changing notions of the communication of faith within the church itself. Among weavers with a background in the revival who have made special contributions to the church are Nancy Jackson of Vallejo, California; Barbara Berg of Decorah, Iowa; and Shirley Herrick of Fridley, Minnesota.

Evidence of religious motivation behind Nordic revival wood-carving is curiously limited, which means that unlike weaving it has left little mark in the church. In *rosemaling*, on the other hand, the area in which the revival has been strongest, reflections of faith have been quite evident. This did not begin with the so-called father of *rosemaling* in America, Per Lysne (1880–1947) of Stoughton, Wisconsin, who seldom if ever included anything of a religious character in his work. An indication of how quickly this changed as the movement progressed is the history of his signature piece, the large wooden serving plate. Ale bowls and tankards had been the serving items most frequently decorated with *rosemaling* in Norway. Lysne realized that these would be little more than decorative items in the American home and developed his large plate with wide flat rim (an object without specific prototype in Norway) on which he painted a *rosemaling* motif in the center and around it the inscription *Smorgaasbordet er nu daekket. Vaer saa god.* [The buffet table is now ready. Help yourself.] This strange mixture of Swedish and Norwegian apparently did not disturb Norwegian or Swedish immigrants who by the 1930s were regularly crossing ethnic lines to marry one another. Lysne sold thousands of these objects, and adaptations of his plate can well be considered the beginning of the revival of *rosemaling* in America. Almost immediately, however, many of Lysne's imitators began choosing alternate inscriptions that would reflect their personal faith. Common substitutions were *Gi os idag vort daglige brod* [Give us this day our daily bread] with spellings reflecting various stages in the development of the Norwegian language, or as much of a Norwegian table prayer, *I Jesu navn gar vi til bords* . . . [In Jesus' name we go to the table . . .], as space would accommodate. Gyda Mahlum of Beloit, Wisconsin, for example, sold hundreds of Lysne-inspired plates, but with Christian inscriptions, at the private museum Little Norway in Blue Mounds, Wisconsin and other places for several decades from the 1950s and on.

Derivations of the Lysne plate, in fact, became the major vehicle for religious expression among rose painters in America. The inscription became a quotation from Scripture and the central motif was usually a free version of the so-called "Telemark rose," a scrolling stem with a suggestion of a root and with secondary stems having flowers and leaves scrolling out from them. Its organic totality and its open, even explosive form can convey feelings of unity, power, joy, and the like; and the inscriptions generally have messages relating to these themes. Judy Ritger of River Falls, Wisconsin has over the past two decades created an impressive number of such plates each of which makes a strong statement of faith, but she is far from alone in this effort. Each of the yearly national competitions in *rosemaling* at Vesterheim generally brings out two or three artists who expand the range of this genre. The example that has received most widespread attention dates from 1992 and is by Norma Getting of Northfield, Minnesota. The inscription is the Norwegian version of Matthew 17:20, which in English translation reads, "And Jesus said unto them, 'Because of your little faith. For truly I say to you, if you have faith as a grain of mustard seed, you will say to this mountain, "Move from here to there," and it will move; and nothing will be impossible to you'" (Fig. 8). In this instance the Telemark rose itself is not only an exceptionally dynamic and radiant one, but it is suspended in what appears to be the ultimate source of power breaking through as rays of light from behind. In a totally different way than Nettie Halvorson's tapestry, this plate, too, epitomizes the abstract expression of faith.

In a bowl created several years before this plate, Getting related the explosive energy of the Telemark rose to creation itself. The classic work making this analogy, however, is the so-called "Genesis bowl" by JoSonja Jansen in which the middle section has the cosmos organizing itself in small spiraling fashion into the centrifugal force that moves the whole cosmos (Fig. 9). Around this floats a series of Telemark roses, depicted as if they are early manifestations of the original force. The total effect is one of cosmic energy having been brought into a dynamic but harmonious unity with the energies of the earth. The inscription relates to God bringing light out of darkness and recognizing that the light is good.

Although *rosemaling* is primarily a floral decoration, figures can be a part of it, and many of the painters in the *rosemaling* revival use pictorial images in making their statements of faith. No common style for doing this, however, has emerged. Each artist has arrived at his or her own idiom. Key figures among them are Susan Toftey of St. Cloud, Minnesota; Irene Lamont of Eau Claire, Wisconsin; Jean Giese of DeSoto, Wisconsin; and Karen Jensen of Milan, Minnesota. Toftey had artistic experience before being exposed to *rosemaling* and was therefore drawn toward the representational. The style of figure found in the biblical scenes of the nineteenth-century Halling painter Nils Baera (1785–1873) gave her a point of departure. Her style carries the decorative elements of *rosemaling* into figure painting in a way that gives it qualities of both the sophisticated and the naive. For figures, Irene Lamont too has developed her style in the grammar of old painting, but she has not had as specific a model as Toftey. She has simply applied the principle of flatness and linearity that generally characterizes naive painting and has presented even contemporary religious subject matter that way. The result is as near as one gets to a truly living contemporary Norwegian folk art, but Lamont's production in work of this type has unfortunately been limited.

For Jean Giese there have long been indications through her choice of texts of a complete integration of the religious into her art. An interesting example of how she saw the Christian faith, language, and art as aspects of her Norwegian heritage is an anniversary plate painted for her country church showing the immigrants bowed from tilling the soil as in Norway but with their newly built church on a hill in the background. Beyond that stands Christ with his comforting message *Kom hit til meg* [Come unto me].[10] The integration of comparatively realistic images and the *rosemaling* elements with their texts that frame the central composition is completely successful. It is as if the artist saw all as part of one world.

Two other painters who do magical things with this integration are JoSonja Jansen and Karen Jenson. A classic example by JoSonja Jansen is her bowl from the early 1990s depicting the good shepherd, in which the flowing robes of the figure pick up the rhythms of the scrolling petals and leaves around them. The halo of the shepherd echoes the sunburst character of the surrounding flowers. The flock of sheep, though something of a contradiction because they are shown in perspective in spite of the comparative flatness of what surrounds them, are also integrated by being painted with feathery decorative brush strokes of rather even size. This is all accomplished without the piece acquiring the character of sheer virtuosity. The shepherd comes across as a personal but secure provider, having as much the character of God the Father himself as of his Son.

Jenson is the most lively and daring interpreter of religious subject matter. While JoSonja Jansen favors the decorative in the union of faith and folk art, Karen Jenson favors the narrative and interpretive. A plate has at its center Adam, fat and decadent from reveling among the Telemark roses of paradise. He is about to meet his Eve who sneaks out of a flower like the serpent itself. The work has a whimsy with which only people totally confident in their faith can risk. In this her work resembles that of folk artists of Mexico. In a nativity bowl, Jenson limited her pictorial subject matter to the center, where she could individualize the character of the figures, including the livestock and poultry, without being overly concerned with the decorative. The wings of the hovering angels in the border, on the other hand, are all but totally integrated into the surrounding scrolls. It is a typical example of Jenson's remarkable imagination and versatility.

The *tour de force* in statements of faith in the *rosemaling* revival is Karen Jenson's canopy bed from 1982 with the full text of the bedtime prayer, "Now I lay me down to sleep," and its morning counterpart running around the interior of its top. The ceiling has panels with the story of redemption as related in Old Testament scenes from the fall of man to the ascension of Elijah. The economy of lines and brush strokes and the vitality of their execution make these a high point in the religious painting of the Norwegian-American arts and crafts revival. The decorative, the expressive, and the representational are brought together here into one artistic whole. The only clearly recognizable *rosemaling* in the ceiling is the wave in the form of an acanthus scroll that carries Jonah's ship and the great fish, and that also sweeps the prophet from the former into the mouth of the latter.

Touches of humor in the panels, like showing the pair of elephants from behind as they enter the ark, are combined with dead seriousness as found in the expulsion from Eden and the ascent of Elijah in the fiery chariot. This makes these early episodes in the spiritual history of humankind a rich, living experience.

"I NEVER THOUGHT OF THE DIFFERENCE"

The present study shows that folk artists in the Norwegian-American communities inherited much more from Norway than stylistic traditions. In many cases an inherited and developing tradition of folk faith informed their work as well. This has helped make their creations into works of genuine folk art, works that result from a personal need to express faith and personal commitment, works that represent the best the individual artist technically and artistically can offer. This can give these works the unique character often considered fundamental to the definition of art.

In the great art of ancient and primitive cultures, religion arose and evolved along with art, the latter transforming the intuitive impulses of faith into form. In the case of the Norwegian-American immigrant artists, a folk faith had been passed down which was, and still is, seeking to find affirmation through pictorial or literary testimony. The view of Norwegian-American people's art that I have offered here by no means, of course, explains it as a totality, but it is one that accounts for much we find in it. Nostalgia, concern with roots, and the sheer aesthetic joy of manipulating forms and colors are certainly present. At the same time, it is filled with the expression of religious faith. I once asked Norma Getting if it has been the religious message of her work or the joy of doing something in the way her ancestors did that has been most important to her, and she said, "I never thought of the difference." Her remark may bring us close to the truth for many Norwegian-American folk artists.

NOTES

[1]*Editor's note*: Marion John Nelson's untimely death kept him from completing this essay. Shortly after his death, Lila Nelson located a nearly complete draft of this article and a number of the illustrations Marion Nelson used when he presented the findings of this essay in an unwritten, informal lecture at *Crossings: Norwegian-American Lutheranism as a Transatlantic Tradition,* in April 1999. In its present form, the article is an edited version of a draft prepared after that event. Always scrupulous in the matter of documentation, Nelson was not able to complete notes for this essay and I have not attempted to provide them except where the author made explicit references to secondary literature or biblical references in his text. Many of the artists discussed here are also examined in more detail in Marion Nelson, ed., *Norwegian Folk Art: The Migration of a Tradition* (New York, 1995). Lila Nelson and Clarence Burton Sheffield, Jr. provided assistance in editing this article as well as in locating illustrations.

[2]Ananda Coomaraswamy, *The Transformation of Nature in Art* (Cambridge, MA, 1934).

[3]Earle Coleman, *Creativity and Spirituality: Bonds between Art and Religion* (Albany, 1998).

[4]C. Kurt Dewhurst, Betty MacDowell, and Marsha MacDowell, *Religious Folk Art in America: Reflections of Faith* (New York, 1983).

[5]Luke 22:21.

[6]*Den Hellige Skrift* (Chicago, 1890). A copy of the example of this Bible used by Christenson remained for some time in the possession of a nephew.

[7]*The Complete English Bible* (London, 1788).

[8]Margit Landsverk Mindrum, *No Change My Heart Shall Fear* (Janesville, WI, 1974).

[9]Psalm 23 and Psalm 123.

[10]Matthew 11:28.

Pastors for the Congregations: Transatlantic Impulses

Vidar L. Haanes

THE FIRST PURPOSE OF THIS ESSAY is to discuss ideals and cultural patterns relevant to the education of ministers brought to America by Norwegian immigrants. It then considers what these immigrants discovered in the United States that shaped the development of their congregational life and their conceptions of the relation between congregations and pastors. It follows their struggles to build schools and seminaries and to educate pastors in light of their evolving ideals. Finally, it tracks impulses and ideas from Norwegian America that crossed the Atlantic eastward and influenced educational patterns in Norway.[1] It is thus a study of transatlantic impulses.

NORWEGIAN PASTORS AND CONGREGATIONS IN THE 1840S

Church historians have traditionally concentrated their energies on leading figures and theological controversies. They have until recently generally neglected sources like sermons, diaries, periodicals, and newspapers that open the way toward understanding the socio-cultural background of participants in interactive relationships and conflicts that shape communities. This is particularly important for understanding both Norway and Norwegian America during the period of the great immigration.

In nineteenth-century Norway there was no aristocracy or ruling class in the strict sense. State officials formed a class of their own, to which the pastors belonged. This was an elite of bureaucrats that administered the country according to the Norwegian constitution of 1814. Yet pastors were unlike other members of this class. Pastors for the most part lived among their peasant parishioners and were thus a link between the state bureaucracy and the people. Pastors formed a class similar to that of American lawyers, whom the European observer Tocqueville described as a political upper class, a conservative and intellectual elite, the functional aristocracy in America.

In Norway the clergy perceived the parish to be an inclusive geographical entity in which civil and clerical boundaries coincided. Ordinary people were expected to behave morally, to attend church on Sundays or at least on the great feast days, and to finance the professionals who did the serious religious work on behalf of the congregation.

Congregations as voluntary organizations

In America congregations are by nature voluntary; they are composed of people who have chosen to congregate. This reflects a principle deeply embedded in the American way of life. In 1830 Tocqueville was struck by the voluntary nature of American religion and by its variety. In America there was no state church to promote the interests of the ruling class. If one wanted to express social or political dissent, one could do so without also abandoning religion. This was quite a new situation for the Norwegian immigrants to the United States. In terms of formal affiliation with religious communities, they were accustomed to the restraints of linguistic, ethnic, and class barriers. Upon arrival in the United States some Norwegian immigrants altogether abandoned organized religious life. Others became Methodists, Baptists, or Mormons. Some joined still other denominations. Most of the Norwegian immigrants, however, celebrated life in the United States because it enabled them to retain beliefs that originated outside of it. They thus could develop what Jon Gjerde calls "complementary identity."[2] Or, as sociologist Steve Bruce puts it: "Americans are religious because the Church offers them a way in which they can display their commitment to American values, while maintaining their ethnic distinctiveness."[3] Gjerde uses the concept of complementary identity in a discussion of "learning republicanism."[4] We might well use the same concept in connection with the Norwegians who learned in America not only how to replace monarchy with republicanism but also of the ways of voluntary congregations and denominations.

Not many Norwegian emigrants left their homeland for religious reasons. They were accustomed to the Lutheran liturgical service, to the associated rites of the church, and to the ministries of a pastor. Other than some Haugeans who had been leaders back home, most of these immigrants had little experience to equip them for leadership in the local congregation. From 1825 to 1844 no ordained ministers from the Church of Norway accompanied emigrants to their new homes in America. After several years of informal association under the leadership of a number of lay leaders, Norwegian immigrants began organizing permanent congregations and denominations in 1843. The Haugean lay preacher Elling Eielsen (1804–1883) was the first Norwegian to be ordained for ministry in the United States, although his ordination later seemed a bit mysterious to the pastors of the Norwegian Synod formed in 1853. Unlike Eielsen, these ministers had been educated and ordained in Norway prior to departing for the United States. Even before they arrived, however, another layman, a young Danish schoolmaster, Claus Lauritz Clausen (1820–1892), was also ordained for service among the Norwegians in America by a German-American pastor of the Buffalo Synod, in 1843. Simmering religious conflict among Norwegian-American Lutherans was not reduced by the arrival on the scene of Pastor Johannes Wilhelm Christian Dietrichson (1815–1883) in 1844. Johannes Dietrichson was an aggressive advocate of state church practice and the use of the official liturgical manual, the *Church Ritual* of 1685. Like others of his class, he had his pride and was ever aware that he belonged to the educated class of higher officials. In Norway this had placed the clergy on a pedestal as the unquestioned authorities in religious and congregational matters. It is especially important to recognize the major class distinction between the congregations and the first pastors of what would become the Norwegian Synod in 1853, all of them coming as they did from "the gentry tradition of noble service," as Leigh D. Jordahl puts it.[5]

Elling Eielsen and some of his close followers continued to think of the Norwegian pastors as unbelieving, blind guides to salvation. The Ellingians thus continued to be highly skeptical toward formal ministerial education. But for most Norwegian immigrants, having left behind their local communities and social structures, the familiar figure of the Lutheran pastor played an important role in easing the transition from Europe to the United States.

ABOUT HIGHER EDUCATION

The question of higher education for the clergy was central to the church struggles of the early Norwegian Americans, as it has been in Norway since the beginning of the nineteenth century. In 1799 Mikkel Hauge, Hans Nielsen Hauge's brother, and his cousin, Paul Gundersen, were out preaching near Tønsberg in Vestfold. One year earlier, the Latin School in Tønsberg had been made into a public school with a rationalistic curriculum based on Enlightenment ideas. Gundersen mentioned this school in a letter, saying: "We have spent two days here, but were hardly allowed to witness for the truth, and what Luther says is right, 'the high schools are wide gates to hell.'"[6]

Did Martin Luther actually say that? Luther, who was himself so proud of his doctorate in theology that he later declared that he would give the whole world for it? Not quite. But in his *Appeal to the Ruling Class of the German Nation* he did say: "Nothing could be more devilish or disastrous than unreformed universities." "What are they but places where loose living is practiced, where little is taught of the Holy Scriptures and Christian Faith, and where only the blind, heathen teacher Aristotle rules, far more than Christ." "The universities only ought to turn out men who are experts in the Holy Scriptures, men who can become bishops and priests, and stand in the front line against heretics, the devil, and all the world. But where do you find that?" "I greatly fear," Luther continued, "that the universities, unless they teach the Holy Scriptures diligently and impress them on the young students, are wide gates to hell."[7] It is important to note that Luther speaks here about unreformed universities, not about higher education as such.

Mikkel Hauge is one of many representatives of the laity in Norway who adopted Martin Luther's critical stance toward higher education. The negative experience of these first Haugeans made a deep impression on later figures like Elling Eielsen. Yet it would be a mistake to take such expressions as negative toward education as such. Hans Nielsen Hauge (1771-1824) himself paid for private Latin lessons for his only son Andreas, then sent him to the Latin school, then to university for theological studies. In 1839, the same year Elling Eielsen arrived in America, Andreas Hauge (1815-1892) graduated from the university as *canditatus theologiae,* and he was later ordained for ministry. The Hauge family represents the social transformation of the peasant class in Norway. Hans Nielsen Hauge's grandson, who bore his grandfather's name, eventually became Dean of Skien and even Minister of Church Affairs in the Norwegian government.[8] The history of the Hauge family charts both the social upheaval of an era and a reorientation of attitude on the part of an entire class in Norway.

The situation is further confused by the complex relations between the early Haugeans and exponents of the views of Nicolai Frederik Severin Grundtvig (1783-1872). J. W. C. Dietrichson, for example, was a Grundtvigian, while Elling Eielsen was among the most radical of Norwegian Haugeans. Clausen was both Grundtvigian and Haugean. And they were all Lutherans. In Norway almost everyone but the old rationalistic clergy supported Grundtvig until 1840. The first two theological professors at Royal Fredrik's University in Oslo, Sven Borchmann Hersleb (1784-1836) and Stener Johannes Stenersen (1789-1835), were both friends and supporters of Grundtvig. Many Haugeans were admirers of Grundtvig and even his personal friends, including, for example, Amund Helland (1786-1870) of Bergen. Hans Nielsen Hauge urged his followers to remain within the state church, but after Hauge's death Grundtvig wrote to Helland in 1826 and told him that the Haugeans in Norway could not have a foot in both camps, one foot in a church governed by infidels, and one in something they wrongly considered a church. Grundtvig said, "The State Church is nothing but the public funeral of the Church."[9]

In 1826 Grundtvig also wrote to his friend in Oslo, Wilhelm Andreas Wexels (1797–1866): "The situation of the Haugeans is desperate. They simultaneously want to be in the Church and outside of it. It is remarkable that no pastors in Norway have the courage to rescue those who will live like Christians . . . and either lead them back in a purified state church, or constitute a pure, Christian congregation with its own theological seminary, what perhaps would create miracles in Scandinavia. If I were Norwegian, I certainly would try something like that."[10] No one in Norway followed up this idea. In the 1820s and 1830s Grundtvig had focused on pastoral education and the need for a sound biblical theology. He always emphasized the primary role of the congregation and the need for a spiritual awakening. Grundtvig's influence would eventually be severely circumscribed in Norway and even more in Norwegian America when, a few years later, confessional Lutherans discovered that Grundtvig had made the "matchless discovery" that the Apostle's creed and the baptismal formula were the "living word" upon which the church stood. Nor did Grundtvig's idea for a seminary built on a foundation of free, living congregations survive long among layfolk or pastors after Professor Gisle Johnson (1822–1894) emerged as the leader of a revival in Norway.

What about universities and the gates of hell in Norwegian America? By this time the people of these churches had begun to evolve a polity that made room for both self-governing congregations and educated pastors. Most immigrants would likely not have said, "Thank God, we are free from the state church and the pastor." Most seem rather to have looked to Norway for assistance. They often tried to obtain pastors trained at the University in Oslo until the time came when they could train their own pastors in their own seminaries. This was mentioned as early as 1852 by Adolph Carl Preus (1814–1878) in his definition of the synod as a free association of congregations for the purpose of church matters. And among these church matters was "education of future pastors and teachers for the service of the

Church."[11] The Norwegians knew only one way of educating pastors, namely, ten years of Latin school, followed by five years in the university. But here Grundtvig appears again. In America, as they had not in Norway, the Haugeans did exactly what Grundtvig had advised them to do in Norway. They attempted to "constitute a pure, Christian congregation with its own theological seminary." Note that Peter Andreas Rasmussen (1829–1898) came from a Haugean home in Stavanger, where this combination of Hauge and Grundtvig was common, and where he had witnessed the beginning of the Stavanger School of Mission. Rasmussen was a member of Eielsen's synod, but went to the practical theological seminary in Fort Wayne, Missouri, for two years. Like most Haugeans, Rasmussen was free of Elling Eielsen's distrust of education. Rasmussen, indeed, began a seminary in Lisbon, Illinois, in 1855 and, after a break with Eielsen, took the lead in founding a Haugean seminary in Red Wing, Minnesota, in 1879.

STAVANGER SCHOOL OF MISSION

The Stavanger School of Mission plays a crucial role in this history and is a nexus of connections between Norway and Norwegian America in matters of theological education. The same group who stood behind the establishment of the Norwegian Missionary Society in 1842 also saw the need for a school for the education of missionaries. Some Moravians and a few Haugeans, like John Haugvaldstad (1770–1850) and Amund Helland, but also the father of P. A. Rasmussen and the father of Sven Gunnersen, both members of the so-called "Augsburg triumvirate" in the United States, were among the pioneers in establishing the Stavanger School of Mission in 1843.

A problem for the west-coast Haugeans was that only one person appeared with a calling to serve as a missionary for this new society, namely the stouthearted theological candidate Hans Paludan Smith Schreuder (1817–1882), a friend and companion of J. W. C. Dietrichson. Schreuder was recommended to the Missionary Society by the Mission Committee in Oslo. This committee was dominated by the clergy, as was most Christian work in the capital. Schreuder was ordained as bishop for foreign missionaries in 1866. His theology and his aristocratic behavior, however, proved difficult for the more democratic, lay-oriented society with which he was collaborating. A few years later Bishop Schreuder was dismissed. He continued as mission bishop, however, supported by a committee in Norway. Typically the Schreuder Mission received support from the Norwegian Synod in the United States. Schreuder's work was continued by Nils Astrup (1843–1919), another member of the Norwegian clerical gentry. His sister Ingeborg Astrup married Laur. Larsen. In 1927 the organization was named "The American Lutheran Mission—Schreuder Mission."[12] The complexities of this history illustrate the intricate web of connections binding Norwegian America to the Norwegian homeland.

Stavanger School of Mission, founded in 1843, is the oldest private seminary in Norway. Its goal was to educate pastors for mission work in South Africa and Madagascar. This school represented in several ways a break with the Norwegian state's monopoly in higher education and especially with the fixed pattern of the education of pastors at the national university. First, it was possible to be a student without the coveted *examen artium,* even without what today would be called a high school education in the United States. Second, the new school was a boarding institution where all the students lived together under the fatherly supervision and strict Christian discipline of their teachers. Third, it was emphasized that the students should reach a clear, thorough, and correct knowledge of God's Word according to the Lutheran confessions. Fourth, candidates were ordained for ministry, and were permitted to use the title mission pastor. They could not serve as pastors in the state church, but were recognized as fit for service in the Evangelical Lutheran Church as such.

DIFFERENTIATION AND SECULARIZATION

In the 1840s, just as Eielsen and J. W. C. Dietrichson began what would become their epochal quarrel, the Norwegian state went through a dramatic change. In 1845 we see the beginning of the transition from a static-hierarchical society to a functional-differentiated society in Norway. In 1845 the Dissenter Law had to a certain degree eliminated the equation between Norwegian and Lutheran identities for individuals, although officials of the state were still required to confess the Lutheran faith and to belong to the state church. The coalition between the political, the religious, and the "scientific," as it can be seen in Norway in the links between the nation-state, the church, and the university, was fundamentally altered so as to reduce the capacity of the state, the church, and the academy to define the goals and values of society. The university reform of 1845 in Norway symbolically illustrates tendencies toward pluralization and secularization. In that year, the university ended its tradition of celebrating the Reformation and the king's birthday. This was explained as a break with the old linkage of university, throne, and altar.[13]

Democratization and political liberalism seemed to point toward a separation of church and state in Norway. Yet nothing happened. The state church system remained unchanged, although small groups of Methodists and Baptists demonstrated that the state church did not possess the sole religious truth. Methodist pastors joined ranks with Søren Kierkegaard (1813-1855) and critics within the state church. Anders Olsen (1837-1923), among these critics, described the state church as a church where "the lords of the world govern and are permitted to do so by the church itself; there clergymen are appointed [who] . . . are blind guides who seek the plush parish more than saving souls from perdition."[14] Even Gisle Johnson, who wielded so molding an influence on the theological students of the era, declared that he was glad not to be a pastor in the state church. In 1849 the radical Labor leader Marcus Thrane (1817-1890) attacked the official religion and accused the clergy of using religion in suppressing common people by deceiving them. His own solution was a separation of state and church, a religion without dogmas, and full freedom of religion. He gave up Norway and emigrated, only to find that most Norwegian Americans practiced the Lutheranism of the homeland.

THE CHURCH OF NORWAY AND THE NORWEGIAN SYNOD

Throughout the nineteenth century the theological faculty of the University in Oslo had a monopoly on the education of the Norwegian

Lutheran clergy. Through the teaching of Professors Gisle Johnson (1822-1894) and Carl Paul Caspari (1814-1892), students in Norway were given a solid foundation combining Lutheran orthodoxy and Pietistic revivalism. This was regarded as a "golden age" of this faculty. Except for Laur. Larsen (1833-1915) and Bernt Julius Muus (1832-1900), however, the founding fathers of the Norwegian Synod graduated before the Johnsonian revival of the 1850s started. Most of them were rooted in the older gentry tradition.[15]

A leading class is usually self-supplying, but in America the pastors of the Norwegian Synod did not have a recognized means for sustaining an elitist, official culture. The question for Norwegian Lutherans was thus whether the elitist requirements for pastoral education could be transferred to an American context. A further question concerned transferring the Lutheran theology of civil authority to an egalitarian society. To train its pastors, the Synod after some debate established a Norwegian professorship at the German-American Missouri Synod's Concordia Seminary in St. Louis. Pastors Niels O. Brandt (1824-1921) and Jacob Aall Ottesen (1824-1904) wrote in a report of a visit to this institution how "unspeakably fine" [*"usigelig skjønt"*] it had been to find such a blessed *planteskole* [literally "seminary"] for their dear Lutheran Church.[16] This alliance, however, was never popular with the people of the congregations, and the ministers of the Norwegian Synod were often portrayed as aristocratic and doctrinaire. The professorial position at Concordia was initially filled by Pastor Laur. Larsen in 1859. Larsen left the post in 1861 when the seminary closed during the Civil War, and went on to become one of the founders and the first president of Luther College. The position at Concordia remained unfilled until 1872 when it was filled by Friedrich August Schmidt (1837-1928), who remained there until the Synod opened its own seminary, Luther Seminary, in Madison, Wisconsin in 1876.

One result of this connection to the Missouri Synod was that in most of the congregations connected to the Norwegian Synod pastors with "Old Lutheran" [*Altlutheraner*] views worked hand in hand with a strong laity, often including many individuals with a Haugean background. Without this help from the Missouri Synod,

Laur. Larsen once said, the Norwegian Synod probably would not have reached absolute purity of doctrine.[17] In the Missouri pastors, like Carl Ferdinand Wilhelm Walther (1811–1887) and Wilhelm Sihler (1801–1885), Norwegians like Preus and Larsen recognized the same "Old Lutheran" theology, combined with the simple, childlike faith that they had seen in Christian Thistedahl (1813–1876), their renowned theologian and teacher at Kristiansand Cathedral School. Thistedahl was the tutor of Gisle Johnson, Herman Amberg Preus (1825–1894), Johan Storm Munch (1827–1908), Laur. Larsen, and many more.[18] They were all called *Thistedahls Hebræere* [Thistedahl's Hebrews]. This remarkable pedagogue set his stamp on a whole generation of students. He himself had been one among very few Norwegian theologians ever to receive the coveted *prae ceteris.*[19] He taught his pupils Hebrew, Greek, and Latin, and subscribed to the leading German theological periodicals. Even the Jewish-born, world famous orientalist Caspari said: "I know some Hebrew, but Thistedahl beats me."[20] For twenty years the best students at the theological faculty were alumni from Kristiansand, and Thistedahl was the reason.[21] Several times Thistedahl was offered a chair at the university, but he regularly refused. He could not leave Kristiansand.

The Norwegian pastors did not meet Missourianism for the first time when they arrived in America. They were already acquainted with the backgrounds of the Franconian Lutherans originally dispatched to the United States by Wilhelm Löhe (1808–1872) and the Saxon Lutherans, eventually led by Walther, who had united in 1847 to form the Missouri Synod. Gisle Johnson had contact with Erlangen and with the Society for Inner Missions in the Sense of the Lutheran Church, which Löhe had built up in the little Bavarian village of Neuendettelsau. Caspari had roots in the strict confessional Lutheran group in Prussia and Saxony, with pastors and scholars like Ernst Wilhelm Hengstenberg (1802–1869) and Andreas Gottlob Rudelbach (1792–1862), the Dane who became bishop in Saxony. In the textbooks we often read about "Caspari and Johnson" as if they were the same person. They cooperated well and agreed in many things. Johnson, however, was influenced by Erlangen pietism, while Caspari fought for historic, conservative, confessional Lutheranism. In faculty matters they often fell out on opposite sides. Most of the pastors in the Norwegian Synod would have gravitated toward the views of Caspari, while Clausen, Muus, August Wenaas (1835–1924) and other Conference people would lean more upon the work of Gisle Johnson. This distinction has been somewhat neglected in the historiography of Norwegian-American Lutheranism.

Neither the Missiouri nor the Norwegian Synod pastors were "high church" in orientation. They were rather "Old Lutherans," working for a repristination of the theology found in *The Book of Concord*. In matters of church polity they considered Wilhelm Löhe guilty of "Romanism," and themselves strove to establish a decentralized, democratic constitution for their churches.[22] They did not, however, advocate congregationalism in a strict sense of the word, because they certainly did not envision congregations independent of any ecclesiastical control. The Norwegian Synod indeed defined itself as consisting of pastors and representatives of congregations. Löhe wrote to the Missourians concerning the seminary at Fort Wayne, which he transferred to the Synod in 1847: "We notice that your synodical constitution, as it has now been adopted, does not follow the example of the first Christian congregation. We have good reason to fear that the strong admixture of democratic, independent and congregational principles in your constitution will do greater damage than the interference of princes and governmental agencies in the Church of our homeland."[23]

The pastors of the Norwegian Synod were, however, sure that the congregations would respect them if they served as the ministers of the Word. Next to the preaching of the Word of God, H. A. Preus said in 1867, the congregational meetings are most important. "When a congregation is first formed, divine service usually takes place in the largest house or in a public schoolhouse. These are sometimes too small to hold more than half the crowd; in that case baptism and communion are held in the house and the sermon in the open air under some trees. . . . It is, after all, of secondary importance where the sermon is preached."[24] Preus even tried to explain in his lectures how wonderful it was for a Lutheran church to be without state leadership. At that moment, however, Norway seemed to have nothing to learn from America.

In the 1850s Professor Gisle Johnson established himself as an extremely influential revivalist preacher. Through Johnson's preaching and teaching, generations of Norwegian clergy were so deeply influenced that a nationwide revival took place within the church. The revival fostered a strong laity, and built the foundation for the church reform movement. The paternalistic, hierarchic system belonged to the past, and the horizontal solidarity crossing old cleavages became the new pattern. Nevertheless, the laity in Norway did not build congregations; they could not elect their own pastors; they had no influence whatsoever on their congregational life, except that they could build prayer-houses and arrange Christian meetings in these premises.

Many pastors who returned from America were frustrated about the situation in the homeland. Among them was Johan Storm Munch (1827-1908), son and namesake of the famous bishop in Kristiansand who belonged to one of the most elite among families in Norway. Munch came to America together with Laur. Larsen and served in the Norwegian synod from 1855-1859. Munch eventually returned to Norway, but found the situation as pastor in the state church unbearable. In 1875 he resigned and with Paul Wettergreen established the Lutheran Free Church in Norway.

Augsburg Seminary and the *Public Declaration*

Augsburg Seminary was begun by August Wenaas, a true disciple of Gisle Johnson. Wenaas even named his son Gisle Johnson. He came to America to build a seminary "just like our good Norwegian School of Mission in Stavanger."[25] Wenaas accomplished much in establishing Augsburg, but this school was soon to be the focus of severe controversy among Norwegian-American Lutherans. Eventually better known than Wenaas were Georg Sverdrup (1848-1907) and Sven Oftedal (1844-1911), both as famous as their brothers in Norway, Jakob Sverdrup (1845-1899) and Lars Oftedal (1838-1900). All four were renowned fighters for parliamentarism, church reform, free congregations, and the right of the congregations to call their own pastors. Both pairs of brothers kept in close contact with each other, and in this instance we can plainly talk about strong transatlantic impulses. On both sides of the ocean there was dispute between the old and the new, the aristocratic and the democratic, the privileged classes and the people.

Pastor Johann C. H. Storjohann (1832–1914), the founder of Seamen's Mission, had originally accepted a call to succeed Wenaas as professor at Augsburg Seminary, but his mother-in-law, "Widow Holmboe" from Bergen, refused to move to America. When Wenaas came to Norway, Storjohann thus had to decline the call to the United States. Storjohann, however, recommended Sven Oftedal. Oftedal accepted, but suggested that Wenaas should ask Georg Sverdrup and Sven Rud Gunnersen (1844–1904) as well.[26] Oftedal arrived in October 1873, Sverdrup and Gunnersen in 1874. The three constituted the so-called "Augsburg triumvirate."

Things got off to a stormy beginning with Sven Oftedal's and August Wenaas's notorious *Public Declaration* against the Norwegian Synod and its so-called "Wisconsinism."[27] This resulted in a tremendous transatlantic commotion.[28] Oftedal and Wenaas charged the Norwegian Synod with an exclusivistic attitude, a rigid rejection of lay activity as an infringement on the pastoral office, contempt for spiritual life in the congregation, an unwillingness to establish a theological seminary in a far from poor community, and finally the Synod's secret pastoral conferences.[29] H. A. Preus replied that the Synod had an earnest concern for the truth and that it looked upon public teaching without a call as a breach of order, except in cases of actual emergency. Finally, the Synod agreed that doctrine was not a clerical but a congregational possession. Sven Oftedal addressed the declaration to every Norwegian in Norway and America, and the strife had extended transatlantic consequences. Professor Frederik Wilhelm Klumpp Bugge (1838–1896) at the theological faculty in Norway came to the Synod's aid in the Norwegian periodical *Luthersk Kirketidende.* He declared that the *Public Declaration* was flawed by endless exaggerations, unfairness, and mendacity.[30]

DEMOCRACY OR ARISTOCRACY?

Sven and Lars Oftedal certainly had their enemies, as Georg and Jakob Sverdrup had theirs. In the transatlantic debate occasioned by the *Public Declaration,* the four aligned themselves against clergy and gentry politicians who believed in the right of a natural aristocracy and an ordained ministry to speak to and for the people.[31] Georg Sverdrup and Sven Oftedal both believed that they had been chosen by God to realize the free, New Testament ideal of congregational life. They felt that the Norwegian *barnelærdom* [elementary Christian instruction], the best gift they brought from their old land, "was overshadowed by the Missouri assertions, while the Norwegian clerical aristocracy, the worst to be brought over the ocean, were preserved for ever so long."[32] These reformers positioned themselves against people whom they thought were trying to reestablish slavery, actual chattel slavery and the slavery of congregations under an authoritarian clergy. In his book *The Democratization of American Christianity,* Nathan Hatch mentions the inspiration religious leaders drew from the rhetoric of political revolution. For these leaders "nothing represented ecclesiastical tyranny more than the . . . clergy with their zeal for the theological systems, doctrinal correctness, organizational control, and cultural influence."[33]

On 14 July 1875 Lars Oftedal joined his brother at the official opening of the new Augsburg Seminary. Storjohann was also there to listen to Georg Sverdrup preach a sermon chock-full of revolutionary rhetoric.[34] Echoes of Bastille Day and perhaps of the Fourth of July were in the air that summer day in Minnesota.[35] Sverdrup began his sermon by referring to the struggle to build this school in the American midwest. He then continued: "And near us, in this moment, lies a distant land, Norway, where there is also a struggle, and there, too, it is all about freedom or bondage for the Church of Christ." After a long period in bondage under the king's power and ecclesiastical power, the people of the earth now rise, and in revenge they turn against their oppressors, screaming "Down with Christ"; we hear a scornful laughter over Christianity and church. On the other side we find the church, screaming: "Away with this liberty, for this is a case of people revolting against the Lord. Thus it shall be smashed with our iron scepter and broken upon the ramparts of Jerusalem." In contrast, Sverdrup said, the friends of Augsburg had gathered as a free people, in a free congregation, with Christ among us. Christ had by no means departed from the congregation, even though the people had been set free.

What about the three guests from Norway present on that festive occasion? The experience of democratic American Christianity without any doubt shaped the thinking of Lars Oftedal, Jakob Sverdrup, and J. C. H. Storjohann. It gave Lars Oftedal a vision for his struggle in Norway for political and religious freedom.[36] This may explain how it was possible to mobilize the pietistic laity on the west coast in Norway to align themselves with Venstre, the party of the left and parliamentarism. Jakob Sverdrup started his work for church reform, especially the congregation's right to elect their own pastor. After his visit to Augsburg Seminary, Storjohann started a seminary in Oslo to educate pastors for America and to make it possible for young men, seminarians without training in the Latin School, to take a theological degree. This was not a great success, but it was a venture. Among the teachers in this school we find Sigurd Odland (1857–1937), later to become professor and the founder of Menighetsfakultetet.

FREE AND LIVING CONGREGATIONS

Georg Sverdrup's slogan was *menighedsmessig presteuddannelse* [the education of pastors in the spirit of free, living congregations]. At this crucial point Sverdrup's ecclesiology differs from that of his teacher Gisle Johnson. In Norway Johnson channeled Christian work and fellowship into home mission groups. Consequently his pietistic approach made the laity in Norway too individualistic to build congregations. Georg Sverdrup later argued that Gisle Johnson's revival hindered church reforms, and Sverdrup was right. Johnson channeled the laity's energy into home mission and not into church reform. The result of this was the emergence of private pietistic associations rather than free, living congregations. The representatives of Gisle Johnson's pietistic revival, Sverdrup said, were so concerned about the case of Christianity that they could not take the risk of leaving it in the hands of the congregations.

Georg Sverdrup fought his battles in America, his land of promise. He desperately hoped that the realization of free and living congregations and a congregational education of pastors would make a model for the Church of Norway to follow. He followed the situation in Norway closely, where his uncle, Johan Sverdrup (1816–1892), who was the leading political figure on the left, became prime minister after the victory of parliamentarism in 1884. Georg Sverdrup's brother Jakob Sverdrup was the leader of the reform movement, and he became Minister of Church Affairs. More victories were to be won in the struggles for a democratic and egalitarian constitution, but not in the struggle for church reforms.

In the 1860s a new Church Commission started its work in Norway, with the mandate to reform the structure of the church. The commission suggested a few things, like parochial church councils, but it resulted in very little actual reform. Georg Sverdrup had the impression that the pastors in Norway supported such church reforms as increased their own power and reduced their burdens and responsibilities. When it came to the heart of the matter, the question of self-governed congregations, the pastors backed out in silence or openly foiled these plans. Sverdrup was more than surprised to find that some pastors, who started their careers as rather radical or liberal in these matters, seemed later to be opposed to practically all changes other than those that might function to increase their own power.

Georg Sverdrup's principal target was Johan Christian Heuch (1838–1904), teacher at the Practical Theological Seminary in Oslo, editor of *Luthersk Ugeskrift,* and from 1889 bishop of Kristiansand. Both Sverdrup and Heuch had been disciples of Gisle Johnson, both were highly intelligent, both were masters of the pen. Sverdrup called Heuch responsible for the crisis in the reform movement, because Heuch had exercised so much influence on the younger pastors. Heuch fought hard against rationalism and liberal theology, but he never questioned the state church structure. He was afraid of any reform whatsoever on that front.

Georg Sverdrup had discerned that the lack of intimate cooperation between the laity and the clergy had been unfortunate for the
Church of Norway. He maintained that this meant that there could
be no congregation, but only isolated workers. This meant that the
clergy often saw work for the kingdom of God as mission work,
as the work of missionaries sent out by the king to evangelize and
work in the congregations. Sverdrup, on the other hand, wanted to
talk about work the congregation might do in cooperation with
and through the elected minister. This is a key question and one, in
my own view, of acute contemporary interest: *"Er kristendommen en
prestesak eller en menighetssak?"* ["Is Christianity a matter for the clergy
or the congregation?"].

THE 1880S

After 1875 modernization accelerated rapidly in Norway. Gisle Johnson
surrendered his chair in systematic theology to the markedly more
liberal Fredrik Petersen (1839-1903). A Norwegian clergyman, Daniel
Thrap (1832-1913), wrote in his diary in November 1880 that Professor
Fredrik Petersen was a disaster for the country. He then continued,
"The clergy have every reason to wish Professor Petersen a chair
among our dear brethren in America, where he could tear down
their cocksure certainty with some of his hazy abstractions."[37]
    In 1881 Principal Edvard Hambro (1847-1909), the father of Carl
Joachim Hambro (1885-1964), president of the Norwegian Parliament,
was going for a walk in Bergen. As he walked he considered the
youth of Bergen who moved to Oslo to study at a university so secularized that he feared for the future of Christianity. "Suddenly," he
wrote, "it struck me that the despised congregation might help."[38]
He mentioned this to his brother-in-law, Deputy Mayor Niels Alstrup
Dahl (1840-1904), and to the bishop, Fredrik Waldemar Hvoslef
(1825-1906). Together these three announced the plan of founding
Menighedsuniversitetet [university of congregations].[39] Nothing came
of this, but a seed had been sown. The idea had been born that it
might be possible to build a university or a theological faculty on
the basis of the congregations. It should also be noted that all three

of these figures were in close contact with the Bergen Friends of Reform, a group connecting the old Grundtvig tradition, the church reform movement, the Sverdrup family, and even Sigurd Odland, who was a student of Hambro's and who became the founding father of Menighetsfakultetet [Seminary of the Congregations].

MENIGHETSFAKULTETET

The relation between theologians and laity at the end of the nineteenth century resembles in many ways the relations of the same segments of the church during the era of the Reformation. There was a great gap between university theology and religious sentiment in the congregations. A certain aristocratization of the university milieu, even in the development of seminaries or academies not associated with the universities, also brings to mind developments at the end of the late Middle Ages.

In 1902–1903 the aging Bishop Heuch publicly warned against the new rationalism among young theologians. In this context he made special mention of the theological professors.[40] Georg Sverdrup then wrote him a letter from America. Twenty years earlier they had fought about the question of church reform and free congregations. In this letter Sverdrup argues that as long as the living congregation left the responsibility of training and calling pastors to the state, the congregation could not honestly ask the Lord to bless it, to make it bear fruit in the service of the congregation. "You just let the state have as many theological faculties as they need, but let the congregation have *Presteskole* [seminary], and let the theological teachers in this seminary be responsible servants of the congregation, instead of irresponsible scholars, of whom German science is sole source and norm."[41]

Debate and conflict had by this time developed between the academic theologians at the University in Norway, on the one hand, and the vast majority of the clergy and the layfolk in the Church of Norway, on the other hand. After Norway gained its freedom and independence from Sweden on the 5th of June 1905, the question of freedom and independence for the church became even more acute.

"Let us have a 5th of June for the church," a slogan said. A political church party was founded that worked to liberate the church from the state. The church reform movement continued to strive for the establishment of a church council that would give the congregations more of a voice in their own affairs and independent legislative authority for the church. The government of the day, however, strongly approved the existing connections between state and church. It therefore seemed vital that any professor appointed to the chair of dogmatics be firmly committed to the doctrinal basis of the church. The government thought otherwise. After a prolonged struggle, Dr. Johannes Ording (1869-1929) was appointed in 1906. Like most scholars of the era, he was influenced by German liberal theology. Most disturbing, however, was the fact that he as teacher of dogmatics in a Lutheran church actually regarded himself as Calvinistic on the question of the sacraments and even distanced himself from the creeds of the church in the matter of christology. It was seen as a violation of the right of self-determination of the church when the government forced through this appointment. The only representative of a biblically conservative and confessional theology at the faculty, Sigurd Odland (1857-1937), professor of New Testament, resigned in protest. Even the Minister of Church Affairs, Christoffer Knudsen (1843-1915), left office, almost causing a cabinet crisis during this turbulent political period when the Norwegian government was negotiating with Sweden on the question of the union soon to be dissolved.

Two days after the appointment of Ording, a committee was established in order to "disseminate information aiming at the common body of churchgoers who did not understand what this ecclesiastical controversy was actually about." One of the main tasks seemed to be the realization of a theological faculty independent of the state. The general secretary of the Norwegian Missionary Society, Lars Dahle (1843-1925), wrote: "If it is not possible for the time being to secure Parliament's participation in giving the Church complete self-government, then the people of the Church have two immediate tasks: (1) Local congregations must secure decisive influence over the election of their clergymen. (2) We must have a theological training for the ministry which is formed, protected and approved by the Church."[42]

On 16 October 1907, an organizational meeting was held, at which time Menighetsfakultetet was constituted as an independent theological institution. In one respect this can be seen as a result of the modernization process in Norway. The seminary, as a free institution without connection to the state, was recognized as an equal alternative to the state university, and thus a result of the freedom and pluralism in a modern nation-state. When rejecting the monopoly of the university in higher education, the advocates of Menighetsfakultetet argued on the basis of modern, democratic principles that the new seminary had been founded on the basis of a broad, popular [*folkelig*] movement respectful of the congregations and the devout laity. Thus they succeeded in bridging the old cleavage between the gentry and the people, the pastor and the congregation. The liberals accepted personal freedom, but not institutional freedom. They argued, and still argue today, that a state church secures the personal freedom of the individual against clerical power. Ironically enough, the modern liberal "establishment" wanted and wants today to keep the premodern, static, and elitist university monopoly. Representatives of this point of view fought against Menighetsfakultetet as a modern, liberal, and democratic institution based on conservative and confessional theology. Sigurd Odland became the first professor of New Testament at the new institution. Edvard Sverdrup (1861–1923), another brother of Georg Sverdrup, agreed to teach church history.[43] The third teacher of the newly founded faculty was Peter Hognestad (1866–1931). Hognestad wrote and spoke "*nynorsk*," contemptuously called the "peasants' language." With the appointment of Hognestad, the new faculty became even more overtly a part of the nationalistic awakening. As a result of the growth of the public school system in Norway at this time, an increasing number of peasants' sons came to study theology, and they typically chose Menighetsfakultetet. Peter Hognestad eventually became bishop of Bergen (1916–1931). The fourth person appointed to the new faculty was the famous Ole Hallesby (1879–1961), who represented the pietistic revivalism. The students rallied around the new seminary in increasing numbers, and since 1930 Menighetsfakultetet, the seminary of the congregations, has been the largest seminary in Norway. The state church, however, remains in place.

TRANSATLANTIC IMPULSES

What then crossed the Atlantic with respect to theological education? First we find that impulses from the Haugeans and Stavanger School of Mission crossed from Norway to America. In the United States these impulses came to expression partly in Lisbon Seminary and explicitly in the founding of Augsburg Seminary, both of them predecessors of today's Luther Seminary in Saint Paul, Minnesota. What returned to Norway? Perhaps most importantly, it was the fundamental principle of congregational freedom as it gradually developed among Norwegians in America and in time returned to Norway. This understanding of congregational freedom was reflected particularly in the emerging polities of the several Norwegian-American Lutheran denominations and in their patterns for the education of candidates for the ordained ministry. Menighetsfakultetet, a seminary for the congregations, was founded in 1907 specifically as a prelude to the church's liberation from the state. Had Georg Sverdrup lived another year, he would certainly have celebrated the foundation of Menighetsfakultetet as a precursor to the separation of church and state, as it had been prescribed by the Church Commission in 1908. Once again, however, reform was rejected by the government and a majority of the provincial boards required to vote on the matter. In retrospect it is probably correct to say that Menighetsfakultetet has contributed to keeping the lay movement within the state church framework, and thus to the continuation of the work of Gisle Johnson and Bishop Heuch, rather than to the realization of Georg Sverdrup's ideals. The cry for reform in Norway, in fact, became an *intermezzo* rather than a prelude, and the once vigorous exchange of transatlantic impulses gradually faded from memory during the course of the twentieth century. Whether such an exchange will be revived in future is, of course, an intriguingly open question in our own increasingly international era.

NOTES

[1]Vidar L. Haanes, *"Hvad skal da dette blive for prester?"* *Presteutdannelsen i spenningsfeltet mellom universitet og kirke, med vekt på modernitetens gjennombrudd i Norge,* KIFO Perspektiv, no. 5 (Trondheim, 1998), 124–235, 477, 506ff.

[2]Jon Gjerde, *The Minds of the West: Ethnocultural Evolution in the Rural Middle West, 1830–1917* (Chapel Hill, 1997), 8.

[3]Steve Bruce, *Religion in the Modern World: From Cathedrals to Cults* (Oxford, 1996), 135.

[4]Gjerde, *The Minds of the West,* 54ff.

[5]Leigh D. Jordahl, "The Gentry Tradition—Men and Women of a Leadership Class," in *Church Roots,* ed. Charles P. Lutz (Minneapolis, 1985), 106.

[6]Paul Gundersen, letter of 3 October 1799 to the friends of Hauge, in Hans Nielsen Hauge, *Christendommens Lærdoms Grunde* (Copenhagen, 1800) 36.

[7]Martin Luther, *To the Christian Nobility of the German Nation concerning the Reform of the Christian Estate* (1520), trans. Charles M. Jacobs and rev. James Atkinson, in *Luther's Works,* 55 vols. (Saint Louis and Philadelphia, 1955–1986), 44:201–207.

[8]Haanes, *"Hvad skal da dette blive for prester?"* 417ff.

[9]Daniel Thrap, *Historisk Tidsskrift* (Kristiania) IV. R., 3 (1906), 431f.

[10]Daniel Thrap, *Historisk Tidsskrift* (Kristiania) IV. R., 3 (1906), 428.

[11]A. C. Preus, "Hvad er en Synode?" *Maanedstidende* 2/4 (July 1852), 13.

[12]Haanes, *"Hvad skal da dette blive for prester?"* 112, 232ff.

[13]Bredo Morgenstierne, *Det Kgl. Fredriks Universitet 1811–1911,* 2 vols. (Kristiania, 1911), 1:235.

[14]Anders Olsen, *Evangelisk Kirketidende* 2 (1873), 26. Cited from Arne Hassing, *Religion and Power: The Case of Methodism in Norway* (Waynesville, NC, 1980), 172.

[15]Congregational and Presbyterian ministers, as well as Episcopalian priests, were also typically of genteel origin, highly trained, and well educated, while Baptist and Methodist clergy were of the people. See Roger Finke and Rodney Stark, *The Churching of America, 1776–1990: Winners and Losers in Our Religious Economy* (New Brunswick, NJ, 1992), 76.

[16]"Indbetretning fra Pastorene Ottesen og Brandt om deres reise til St. Louis, Missouri; Columbus, Ohio; og Buffalo, New York," *Kirkelig Maanedstidende* 2 (1857), 481. Cf. "Report of Pastors Ottesen and Brandt on Their Visit to St. Louis, Missouri; Columbus, Ohio; and Buffalo, New York," in Carl S. Meyer, *Pioneers Find Friends: Luther College Lectures, February 21, 22, 1962, Decorah, Iowa* (Decorah, IA, 1963), 70.

[17]Karen Larsen, *Laur. Larsen: Pioneer College President* (Northfield, MN, 1936), 106.

[18]Haanes, *"Hvad skal da dette blive for prester?"* 131ff.

[19]*Laudabilis prae ceteris* [praiseworthy above all others], the highest possible grade given in a Norwegian university. When a candidate received this grade, it was always reported directly to the King.

[20]Åge Holter, *Det norske Bibelselskap gjennom 150 år* (Oslo, 1966), 290.

[21]I am an alumnus of this cathedral school myself, but I had no Thistedahl to teach me Latin or Hebrew. This is the school where Herman Amberg Preus's (1825-1894) father, Paul Arctander Preus (1779-1867), was instructor. Herman Amberg (1754-1837), after whom H. A. Preus was named, was the headmaster.

[22]H. A. Preus, "De kirkelige Forholde blandt de Norske i Amerika," *Luthersk Kirketidende* 9 (1867), 15ff., 43, 129; cf. *Vivacious Daughter: Seven Lectures on the Religious Situation among Norwegians in America,* ed. and trans. Todd W. Nichol (Northfield, MN, 1990), 49ff., 58, 114.

[23]Carl S. Mundinger, *Government in the Missouri Synod* (St. Louis, 1947), 199.

[24]Preus, "De kirkelige Forholde," 57. Cf. Nichol, *Vivacious Daughter,* 73.

[25]August Wenaas, *Livserindringer fra Norge og Amerika,* Bibliotheca Norvegiæ Sacræ 12 (Bergen, 1935), 118, and Haanes, *"Hvad skal da dette blive for prester?"* 199ff.

[26]Sven Rud Gunnersen was the son of a Haugean from Stavanger. As a theological student he lived in the house of Gisle Johnson. He served as Storjohann's assistant in London in 1869. He was a professor at Augsburg 1874-1883, and later a professor at Red Wing 1883-1884. He returned to Norway in 1884.

[27]The Norwegian Synod was sometimes referred to as the "Wisconsin Synod" because of the number of its congregations in Wisconsin in the early years. Likewise its teaching was sometimes referred to by its opponents as "Wisconsinism." The Norwegian Synod is not, however,

to be confused with the more properly so-called "Wisconsin Synod," a German-American body.

[28]Andreas Helland, *Augsburg Seminar gjennem Femti Aar* (Minneapolis, 1920), 440ff.

[29]E. Clifford Nelson and Eugene L. Fevold, *The Lutheran Church among Norwegian-Americans: A History of the Evangelical Lutheran Church,* 2 vols. (Minneapolis, 1960) 1:249.

[30]F. W. Bugge, "Professorerne Oftedals og Weenaas's 'aabne Erklæring,'" *Luthersk Kirketidende,* n. s., 11 (1874), 163.

[31]Haanes, *"Hvad skal da dette blive for prester?"* 205f. and Berge Furre, *Soga om Lars Oftedal,* 2 vols. (Oslo, 1990), 1:210ff.

[32]"Den norske Barnelærdom som er den fortrinligste Gave som vi har med os fra det gamle Land, maatte træde i Skygen for Satserne fra Missouri, medens det norske Embedsaristokrati, som er det sletteste nogen kan bære over Havet, søgtes bevaret i det længste." *Professor Georg Sverdrups Samlede Skrifter i Udvalg,* ed. Andreas Helland, 6 vols. (Minneapolis, 1909–1911), 4:90.

[33]Nathan Hatch, *The Democratization of American Christianity* (New Haven, 1989), 170.

[34]Sverdrup, *Samlede Skrifter,* 3:93–97.

[35]July 14 is, of course, Bastille Day. 1875 was the centennial year of the Battles of Lexington and Concord, the skirmishes that began the American Revolution.

[36]Furre, *Soga om Lars Oftedal,* 210, and Haanes, *"Hvad skal da dette blive for prester?"* 217f.

[37]Diaries of Daniel Thrap, RA (National Archive in Oslo) 4A07711 Ms 8vo, 28–32 (29. November 1880).

[38]N. A. Dahl, Edv. Hambro, and J. W. Hvoslef, *Om et Menighedsuniversitet i Bergen* (Bergen, 1883), 137.

[39]Cf. Vrije Universiteit, the free Calvinist University in Amsterdam, founded in 1880 by Abraham Kuyper (1837–1920).

[40]J. C. Heuch, *Mod Strømmen* (Kristiania, 1902) and *Svar* (Kristiania, 1903).

[41]Georg Sverdrup in letter to Heuch, 12 March 1903 (University Library, Oslo, Brevsamlingen, Number 131). Note the quotation from the *Formula of Concord,* Epitome 1, in *The Book of Concord: The Confessions*

of the Evangelical Lutheran Church, ed. and trans. Theodore G. Tappert et al. (Philadelphia, 1959), 464.

[42]Lars Dahle, *Vor Kirkes Stilling: Hvad bør gjøres?* Smaaskrifter om kirkens Ret og Frihed VIII (Christiania, 1906), 26

[43]James S. Hamre, *Georg Sverdrup: Educator, Theologian, Churchman* (Northfield, MN, 1986), 19f.

"More than the Lord's Prayer": The Black Book Minister on the Prairie

Kathleen Stokker

> "He firmly believed that pastors had the 'Black Book' in their possession, and could do whatever they chose, and that there was nothing under the sun they did not know."[1]

SPOKEN ABOUT JENS KNUDSEN, a character in Peer Strömme's Norwegian-American novel of 1893, *Halvor: A Story of Pioneer Youth*, these words epitomize the power attributed to the Black Book minister, traditionally said to know "more than the Lord's Prayer."[2] Norwegian legends of the Black Book minister, striking in their ubiquity, portray a wide variety of named clergymen using the magical tome to conjure up the devil and force him to do their bidding.[3] In previous work I have interpreted these legends metaphorically, as an expression of pastoral authority. I have also linked the motifs of these legends to specific aspects of Lutheran theology of the scholastic era.[4]

The present article explores the actual existence of the Black Books as compilations of formulas to address everyday problems and especially medical ills. It investigates the extent to which ministers actually owned the Black Book, as legend so persistently suggests.[5] It also briefly surveys medicine's place in the life of the clergy, in both Norway and Norwegian America. Three main issues will be addressed here: the background in Norway for the clergyman's image as a healer, the extent to which the pastor acted as a physician in both

Norway and the American Midwest, and how the minister came to play the role of healer in each country. The article also suggests ways the clergy's medical activity may have contributed motifs to the legends of the Black Book minister.

THE MINISTER AS HEALER IN NORWAY

The image of the pastor as a healer suffers no lack of historical precedent, arising as it does from archaic conceptions of disease as caused by evil powers that could be overcome by a sufficiently strong counterforce. Thus the ancient Greeks prayed to gods and goddesses for relief from disease, while in their temples priests and priestesses who served these deities distributed healing potions to the ailing. The New Testament frequently depicts Christ as a healer, and the tradition associating religion and healing continued in the Christian church. After Christianity arrived in medieval Norway, monasteries played a key role in mediating this pattern. In fact, cloisters provided almost all institutional health care in medieval Norway. At these monasteries clerics cultivated medicinal herbs, and in the cities of Oslo, Bergen, Trondheim, Stavanger, Tönsberg, and Hamar they operated charitable infirmaries.[6] Scandinavia's first medical book, the thirteenth-century *Liber Herbarum* [*Book of Herbs*] produced by the Danish cleric Henrik Harpestreng (1164-1244) appeared in just such a monastic setting.

In view of this background, Oskar Garstein concluded that Norway's oldest Black Book, the late-fifteenth-century *Vinjeboka* [*The Vinje Book*], was probably compiled by a Roman Catholic priest.[7] The magic of the Black Books could be black or white, enabling the user either to harm or to heal. Many of the methods its formulas propose derive from ancient sources including the Greek magical papyri. Rather than eradicating the belief that magic could overcome disease, the coming of Christianity actually added new items to the magical repertoire, investing the sign of the cross, Christ's name, the Bible, clerical vestments, graveyard soil, and the lead from church bells with potent healing powers. Black Book formulas employ all of these means to enhance their magic.

Although the magical view of illness persisted through the Middle Ages, during the Renaissance a competing view began to circulate as well. The herbal healing manual, *En skön lystig ny Urtegaard* [*A Beautiful, Merry New Herb Garden*], by the Dane Henrik Smid (ca. 1495-1563), appeared in 1546 and contended that healing was a revelation from God and that sickness was a part of God's divine plan, with each healer acting as a kind of prophet.[8] The book attained widespread popularity, appearing in frequent reprints up through the 1870s. The magical view of illness as caused by evil and overcome by supernatural incantations nevertheless endured long after the Reformation. This is attested by, among other things, Black Book formulas incorporating Lutheran hymns.[9] Clearly this magical thinking contributed to the image of the Black Book minister, but could not the medical role of the clergy, which also continued after the Reformation, have played a vital role as well?

Clerical healing activities, indeed, not only outlasted the Middle Ages, they expanded in scope in the early modern era. The Norwegian laws of King Christian V (1646-1699) promulgated in the years after 1687 fortified the clergy's medical role by assigning ministers the duty of visiting and treating the sick in their parishes. Physicians, by contrast, received no mention at all in the law, which further placed upon the clergy responsibility for teaching midwives how to conduct themselves in their work.[10] Pursuant to these laws, several early-eighteenth-century ministers, notably Niels Schytte (1692-1739) and Niels Jensen (1693-1764), developed a strong interest in medicine that they passed down to their sons along with their respective pastoral calls.[11] Both sons went on to develop reputations as talented doctors: Erik Gerhard Schytte (1729-1808) together with his wife converted their Bodö parsonage into a hospital,[12] while Niels Jensen's son, Peder Harboe Hertzberg (1728-1802), gained fame in Hardanger as *potetpresten* [the potato minister], significantly improving the level of his parishioners' health by overcoming their long-entrenched refusal to eat this vegetable.[13] He, in turn, passed his medical interest on to his own son, the renowned pastor Niels Hertzberg (1759-1841), who for fifty years functioned in his Hardanger parish as both doctor and surgeon.[14]

Far into the nineteenth century professional medical care remained a rarity for most Norwegians. Distances and the expense of consulting a trained physician presented great obstacles. Instead, the clergy regularly provided their parishioners with the necessary medical assistance. As formal medical education became more accessible, and eventually required, some ministers built upon the healing skills they had learned from their fathers and pursued during university study, usually in Copenhagen. Indeed, many clergymen felt equally as drawn to medicine as to theology, but ultimately chose the ministry because it provided a more secure living.[15] Doctors had not yet acquired the prominent social position they would later earn, nor had medicine advanced to a level meriting public confidence. Even after the passage of the first official step toward medical professionalism, the 1794 *kvaksalverloven* [quack law] forbidding those without formal training from practicing medicine, most Norwegians avoided professional doctors.[16] In addition to expense, long distances, and lack of demonstrable positive effect from early professional treatment, popular attitudes toward disease as ordained by God played a decisive role. Many viewed seeking a doctor's care as a form of interference with God's divine plan. This attitude may be reflected in legends that equate the Black Book's cures with the conjuring up of the devil.

Thus, in a report from the Norwegian Chancellory of 1803, the physician Alexander Möller (1762–1847) complained that his patients "saw disease as divine retribution for their sins which would not be cured without their own and the minister's prayers and supplication."[17] The view of health as being in God's hands was shared by the *kondisjonerte* [professional] and *almue* [peasant] classes alike, but for those of the peasant class, the difference in social class between them and the physician provided further reason for potential patients to avoid the physician.

Coming from a different social background and feeling a duty to defend the newly forming professional standards, many physicians reacted judgmentally, voicing criticism when they encountered the outmoded health practices in the countryside. While ordinary folk felt similarly alienated from the minister as well, as is seen in legends mentioning the minister's very possession of the mysterious and potentially dangerous Black Book, the notion of disease as a function of God's providence served to enhance the clergy's role in healing. This was sustained by the corollary belief that the minister's supplications constituted an effective, even necessary, ingredient in achieving a cure.

The minister, by dint of his own personality or training, moreover, was in many cases better attuned to his parishioners' psychology. During the period when *radesyken* [a syphilis-like disease] raged in Setesdal, for example, Christian Thorn Aamodt (1770–1836) managed to gain the confidence of his afflicted parishioners, though they had previously rebuffed a physician's care. Obtaining medicines and training from the physician in the nearby city of Kristiansand, Aamodt returned to his parish to treat those who had confessed to being infected with the disease.[18]

The greater confidence enjoyed by the clergy also played a role in fighting the smallpox epidemic that raged through the country early in the 1800s. Realizing the minister's privileged position in this regard, the authorities granted ministers a dispensation from the quack law, enabling them to vaccinate their parishioners without fear of legal reprisal. "Doctors," wrote Niels Hertzberg, "would not as soon have gotten popular opinion on their side as ministers—even though this was an illness that everyone was deathly afraid of."[19] While many other self-taught physicians were taken to court for quackery, ministers rarely suffered the same fate. This is suggested, perhaps, by the Black Book minister legend motif that those who use the Black Book normally pay for its power with their very souls, while the Black Book minister uses it with impunity, having tricked the Devil into taking his shadow instead.[20]

The popular view of illness as a combination of magic and God's plan did not change until the development of modern medicine, which had barely begun in 1850 and was not yet complete at the end of the nineteenth century. It was with this "magico-Christian" view of illness that emigrants of the common class left Norway for America.

The minister as healer in Norwegian America

Along with their inherited view of illness, many Norwegian immigrants apparently brought the expectation that they would receive health care from the minister's family. Surprised by this expectation, twenty-one-year-old Elisabeth Koren (1832–1918), the wife of the pioneer pastor of the Washington Prairie, Iowa congregation, reported in her diary on 25 January 1853 having asked a parishioner "whether there were not some other people, older, more experienced" who might be consulted. The parishioner responded that "it would hardly be of any use to go to others if [the pastor's family] did not know what to do."[21] And consult her they did. Elisabeth Koren's diary documents numerous occasions on which parishioners came to her for medical help and advice.[22] It was even falsely rumored in the community that "Vilhelm [her husband] had trained as a doctor."[23]

Having no such training in reality, Elisabeth Koren, like so many other contemporary Norwegian immigrants, made frequent use of the "Doctor Books," nineteenth-century successors to the medieval books by Harpestreng and Smid noted above. Caja Munch (1830–1898), whose husband had come from Norway to serve a parish in Wiota, Wisconsin, writes on 12 August 1857: "We managed as well as we could, read in the medical handbooks and used everything suggested there that we could get hold of." Like Elisabeth Koren, Caja Munch found that "everybody around here turns to us when something is the matter."[24]

Of the pioneer ministers' wives, the most professional caregiver was Oline Muus (1839–1922) in Minnesota, whose husband served Goodhue County's Holden parish and later founded St. Olaf College. She brought a medicine chest for the home and medical instruments along from Norway. Before leaving Norway she had, indeed, learned how to do blood-letting and to assist in medical emergencies from her brother-in-law, a physician. We hear in her letters of a young man being cared for at the parsonage and of her healing activities out in the community. Oline Muus, in fact, became an active health care provider in America and was recognized as such when she received payment for her services.[25]

Not only the parsonage wives, but some pioneer clergymen themselves provided their parishioners with medical care. Claus Lauritz
Clausen (1820–1892), who founded Iowa's St. Ansgar settlement in
1853, assisted his parishioners in this way. "[W]e never had a doctor
and no medicines," recalls one of his parishioners. "Rev. Clausen
helped those who were sick as far as he was able."[26] Necessity, indeed,
often pressed pioneer clerics into service. Occasionally, just as in
Norway, the medical authorities realized and utilized the ally they had
in the clergy. So it was that Pastor Realf Ottesen Brandt (1859–1927)
went into temporary medical practice when smallpox threatened his
Dakota Territory parish in the 1880s. Thalette Mathilde Brandt writes:
"My husband had a talk with the doctor at Estelline and brought
back a supply of vaccine points. Many people, old and young, came
to the parsonage for free vaccination."[27] Again paralleling the experience of Norwegian clergy, some prairie pastors might just as easily
have chosen to be doctors. Nils Endreson Böe (1846–1925) frequently
said so, and eagerly treated his parishioners who often came to him
before consulting a physician.[28] "Whether it was faith or the medicine itself is hard to say," Böe's daughter observes, "but it was really
remarkable how many cases he helped."[29]

The ground for confidence in the clergy's medical activity in
Norwegian America, as in Norway, was trust. In the middle of the
nineteenth century American physicians enjoyed no better repute
than their Norwegian counterparts. Delivering the presidential address at the 1856 annual meeting of the Wisconsin State Medical
Society, John Mitchell could make the sweeping statement that "perhaps no profession, art, or even trade is looked upon with as much
distrust as that of medicine."[30] As in Norway, medical officials on
the prairie decried their patients' attitude toward disease. A typical
complaint appeared in the 1882 Wisconsin State Board of Health annual report, singling out the Norwegians for being next to impossible to treat because they trusted "too extensively to the preachers'
rather than the doctors' directions."[31]

This trust could sometimes prevail even over the divisive doctrinal
disputes that racked the immigrant church. Such was the confidence
placed in Jens Martin Dahl (1836–1906), a minister of the Norwegian

Synod. Laurence M. Larson writes in *The Log Book of a Young Immigrant* that "even those who were actively opposed to the Synod and re- garded Dahl as a blind guide in spiritual affairs, sought his parson- age in quest of healing or sent for him to visit their sick relatives." Although Dahl had training in the rudiments of homeopathic medi- cine, Larson suggests that it was rather his cheerfulness and the way his broad countenance radiated hope and assurance that won him ad- herents. "He understood his people, he could look into their troubles, he could explore their imaginations."[32]

THE BLACK BOOK ON THE PRAIRIE

Given the Norwegian-American minister's vital role in dispensing medical care, we might expect to hear that he had the Black Book. After all, certain lay folk healers among the immigrants, notably Knut Haaga in Coon Prairie, Wisconsin, and Peder Enger in Spring Grove, Minnesota, were identified as Black Book practitioners by the first historians of the early settlements. About Haaga, Hjalmar Rued Holand writes: "In the early years, Coon Valley had no medical help. The nearest doctor lived 150 miles away. People resorted to family remedies . . . and 'homemade doctors.' Hans Haaga from Haagadalen was one of these . . . [and] people maintained that he had *Svarteboka* [The Black Book] and could understand it. Although many were of the opinion that this mystical knowledge was very risky business, others gave him even greater respect."[33]

The ambiguous view people held of individuals said to own the Black Book also surfaces in O. S. Johnson's description of Peder Enger who emigrated from Sigdal, Norway in 1861: "It is said of Peder Enger that he knew more than the Lord's Prayer. . . . [P]eople thought he must be in possession of the Black Book, which could cure this or that ill, but since Peder Enger only did well towards his fellow beings, he could not have had the devil in his service."[34] These accounts leave no doubt that an awareness of the Black Book and its lore had accompanied the immigrants to America. Yet except for Peer Strömme's allusion to the Black Book minister, referring to a character who on the novel's previous page is described as "dreadfully ill-informed," no folklore or other accounts exist associating the Black Book with the Norwegian-American minister.[35]

The lack of Norwegian-American Black Book minister lore is significant. Its absence illuminates both the nature of Black Book minister legends in Norway and the difference between relations of pastors to people as they had existed in Norway and as they developed in America. A recent Norwegian study of Black Book minister legends shows that of the Norwegian ministers who had distinguished themselves as dispensers of medical care, none appear among those identified as owners of the mysterious Black Book. In fact, relatively few Black Book minister accounts specifically portray the minister as a medical practitioner, and those that do tend to treat medical activity ambiguously. The evidence suggests that while the minister's healing activity may have renewed the Black Book legends' timeworn motifs in the ways suggested above—for example, the motif of the minister's using the Black Book with impunity—the ambiguity the legends express toward the minister's power seems to have been a more important factor than his healing activities, that is, actually using the Black Book or other medical manuals in these legends' formation. The example of Hermann Ruge, parish pastor of Slire in Valdres from 1737 to 1763, proves illustrative. As befits a Black Book minister, Ruge was said to be "one of the most outstanding ministers who has ever served Slire . . . and an exceptionally learned man, one of the most learned in his time." About Ruge the local dean of the clergy writes: "He had some training in medical matters, too, and took in at the parsonage as many ailing people as he had room for and more—to give them medical treatment. Indeed, his home more resembled a hospital than a parsonage, and many were cured there by his doctoring. Nevertheless, people did not believe so much in his medicine and doctoring skills. Instead they knew that he had studied at Wittenberg and that he had the Black Book, and could make the devil dance, if he wanted, and that it was with this help that he could heal."[36]

To this physician-minister, distinctly unlike those mentioned in the first half of this article, the people attributed the use of the Black Book. For Ruge's parishioners, apparently, his superior education, extended study abroad, and his upper-class way of life created and sustained a distance between them that his efforts as a healer could not overcome. In seeking reasons for his parishioners' willingness to attribute his talents to the Black Book, we need look no farther than the description provided by the local dean, who continues: "He was an excellent farmer and ran the large Slire parsonage well. He worked hard to get people to plant potatoes. But he also drove his twelve cotters [*husmenn*] rather hard, something they hadn't been used to in Abested's [his predecessor's] time. Then they had learned to be quite lazy . . . so the cotters didn't think so much of the new pastor."[37] The alienation of these eighteenth-century cotters from their hard-driving pastor apparently disposed them to regard all aspects of the minister's activity, including his efforts to heal them, with suspicion, as expressed in the time-appropriate image of his possessing the Black Book.

During the nineteenth century, the attribution of magic to their ministers by the common folk of Norway began to wither due to increasing education, industrialization, and professionalism. The distance separating the minister's education and lifestyle from those of his parishioners, a distance already diminishing in Norway, receded even further as the immigrants settled into the American way of life. Certainly the parishioners' changed view of their minister, which considered him less a wizard than an ordinary person, helps account for the lack of Black Book minister lore on the prairie. Perhaps even more significant, however, was the diminishing distance in the *relationship* between the minister and his congregation, a rapprochement that came more swiftly in the American context than in the Norwegian.

Articulating almost to the point of caricature the old European gulf between the the common folk and the upper-class minister, Caja Munch, in a letter dated 22 January 1856, expresses her disdain for "these silly peasants, who for the most part cannot comprehend at all that we are a step above them and have more requirements. No, they regard themselves maybe fully as high and always say *Du* [the familiar form of address], and many such things, which sometimes really are highly ridiculous. . . . For example many will simply call me Caja."[38] Not surprisingly, Caja Munch and her husband soon and with relief resumed residence in Norway. Voicing a sharply contrasting view, a Wisconsin resident details in a letter of December 1878 the new and in his eyes "more desirable" relationship between pastors and their congregations that he finds characteristic of the new land: "One does not fear the pastor other than as a messenger pointing to the Lamb of God who bears the sins of the world. He is not an aristocrat. One dares to speak to him and ask him about everything. There can be no doubt that the pastors are in a better position to counsel people here than in the Norwegian state church."[39] The greater openness that this and other observers say characterized the relationship between the Norwegian-American clergy and their congregations seems to have removed a measure of the parishioners' ambiguity toward their pastor and his power. The persistence of this element of ambiguity, rather than the minister's particular activities, medical or otherwise, helps to explain the durability of the legends of the Black Book minister in Norway. On the other hand, the resolution of this ambiguity in Norwegian America helps explain why no such legends arose about Norwegian-American ministers despite the fact that such legends continued to be told about some of their Norwegian counterparts, as well as about contemporary Norwegian-American folk healers.

The combination of changing times and increasing enlightenment, but above all more comfortable relations between pastor and parishioners, removed the basis for developing a Norwegian-American lore of the Black Book minister. Yet, as we have seen above, many a prairie pastor, although no longer assisted by the magical Black Book and drawing instead upon his psychological insight and willingness to serve his parishioners where and how they needed him most, nevertheless continued to know and to provide "more than the Lord's Prayer."

NOTES

[1] Peer Strömme, *Halvor: A Story of Pioneer Youth,* trans. Inga B. Norstog and David T. Nelson (Decorah, 1960), 37.

²A typical formulation appears in K. Weel Engebretsen and Erling Johansen, *Sagn fra Östfold* (Oslo, 1947), 104: "There is talk of several ministers at Heie, who knew somewhat more than the Lord's Prayer." Unless otherwise noted translations from the Norwegian are the author's.

Tore Bergstöl reports in *Atterljom: Folkeminne fraa smaadalene kring Lindesnes,* 2 vols. (Oslo, 1930), 2:22: "There were many in the old days who had the Black Book, especially ministers. It was copied from the Seventh Book of Moses." About the *Seventh Book of Moses* (which tradition equally often refers to as the *Sixth Book of Moses* or as *Cyprianus*), Joh. Th. Storaker says in *Sagn og Gaader* (Oslo, 1941), 24: "The *Sixth Book of Moses* has by the learned been left out of the Bible, so that common folk shall not get to know what it contains. Those who used it correctly could do amazing things such as no mere mortal could accomplish." Storaker adds: "His arts he had learned at the Black School in Wittenberg which he had attended" (17). I have elsewhere explored the implications of this tradition's invocation of Luther's university and the suggestion that Lutheran efforts obscured rather than revealed Scripture as Luther had originally intended them to do. See note 4 below.

³Almost every district in Norway had a remarkable minister about whom these legends were told. An awareness of this lore certainly accompanied the Norwegian emigrants to America. An informal analysis I have conducted of death dates for ministers identified in the legends as having the Black Book shows their deaths to span the years from 1577 to 1883.

Most of the Black Book minister legends fall into seven major story-types, told in numerous variants all around the country. Reidar Christiansen identified six of these types (ML) in his legend catalogue, *The Migratory Legends* (Helsinki, 1958): ML 3000—Escape from the Black School, in which the minister tricks the devil into taking his shadow instead of his soul as payment for instruction in the black arts; ML 3005— The Would-Be Ghost, in which the Black Book minister causes a parishioner who comes to spy on him to sink into the ground, allowing him to resurface only if he "confesses" his identity; ML 3010—Making the Devil Carry the Cart, in which the minister, who has an enormous parish, but whose carriage has broken down, conjures up the devil to provide transport; ML 3015—The Card Players and the Devil, in which the Black Book minister exorcises the devil who has come to haunt the card players and refuses to leave; ML 3020—Inexperienced Use of the Black Book, in which a servant or other unauthorized user of the Black Book gets hold of the magical tome, conjures up the devil, and must be rescued by the minister; ML 3025—Carried by the Devil, in which the minister conjures up the devil to carry him with supernatural speed to a distant place. To these I have proposed adding ML 3007.5—Catching the Thief, the equally widespread account of the minister being able to "bind and loose" a thief at will. See Kathleen Stokker, "To Catch a Thief: Binding and Loosing and the Black Book Minister," *Scandinavian Studies: Nordic Narrative Folklore* 61 (1989), 353-374.

[4]Stokker, "To Catch a Thief"; "ML 3005—'The Would-Be Ghost': Why Be He a Ghost? Lutheran Views of Confession and Salvation in Legends of the Black Book Minister," in *Arv: Scandinavian Yearbook of Folklore* 47 (1991), 143-152; and "Between Sin and Salvation: The Human Condition in Legends of the Black Book Minister," in *Scandinavian Studies* 67 (1995), 91-108.

[5]As the folklorist Joh. Th. Storaker suggests in *Sagn og gaader,* 18: It is not unreasonable that ministers would have owned the Black Book: "There was a time when even more copies of the infamous book (*Cyprianus*) were spread in not so few copies around the communities, such that it would not be so strange if it found its way onto the minister's bookshelf. A reliable source has told the undersigned that after the last in the series of pastors who bore the family name 'Schive' and served at Bjelland, a sale was held including [the legendary Black Book Minister] Sören Schive's book collection, whereof . . . two editions of this book, filled with prayers and formulas—both a German and a Norwegian edition. . . ."

[6]The Council of Tours in 1163 stated that the church does not shed blood, and that utterance practically forbade the clergy from occupying themselves with medicine. A decree of Pope Celestine V (1214-1296), however, expanded the range of help that priests could give with regard to internal diseases to include the poor, in addition to relatives. As a result, general care of sick people in cloisters and infirmaries became permissible and probably also included care of people other than the poor. See Per Holck, "The Very Beginning: Folk Medicine, Doctors and Medical Services," in *The Shaping of a Profession: Physicians in Norway Past and Present,* ed. Öyvind Larsen and Bent Olav Olsen (Canton, MA, 1996), 29-30.

[7]Oskar Garstein, ed., *Vinjeboka: Den eldste svartebok fra norsk middel-alder* (Oslo, 1993).

[8]Smid's book was about the preparation of medicines from herbs, essentially a translation of Hieronymus Bock, *Krautterbuch*, which first appeared in Strassburg in 1539 and was reissued in 1546. See I. Reichborn-Kjennerud, "En oversigt over og karakteristik av de gamle nordiske læge-böker," *Tidsskrift for den Norske Lægeforening: Tidsskrift for praktisk medisin*, n.s., 44 (1924), 425.

[9]Luther's own beliefs in the existence of tangible demonic spirits, of course, also attests to the persistence of magical thinking.

[10]Per Holck, "The Very Beginning," 32.

[11]The Enlightenment, which performed an enormous service for folklore by encouraging the clergy to write descriptions of their parishes including popular customs, also advanced the idea that improving the people's standard of health constituted an integral part of the clergy's task. Something of the international nature of these views is documented by George Herbert (1593-1653), who in *The Country Parson* identifies as one of the three responsibilities of the parson's wife: "curing and healing of all wounds and sores with her own hands which skill either she brought with her or he takes care she shall learn by some neighbor." See *The Country Parson and The Temple*, ed. John W. Wall, Jr. (New York, 1981), 68. About the pastor in his circuit Herbert says: "If curing poor people, he supplies them with Receipts [medical formulas] and instructs them further in that skill showing them how acceptable such works are to God and wishing them ever to do the cures with their own hands and not to put them over to servants" (75). This latter injunction is of interest given the common Black Book minister legend of a servant finding the minister's Black Book and, to his peril, inadvertently using it to loose the devil. See note 3 above in regard to ML 3020.

[12]Olav Bö, *Folkemedisin og lærd medisin: Norsk medisinsk hverdag på 1800-tallet* (Oslo, 1986), 303.

[13]Peder Harboe Hertzberg's interest in folk medicine may also be seen in his book describing the healing mineral spring at the Finnås parsonage, the waters of which he also used in his cures. See Bö, *Folkemedisin og lærd medisin*, 26.

[14]In addition Hertzberg vaccinated his parishioners for smallpox in 1803, just a few years after Edward Jenner's pioneering paper on the

subject. Hertzberg's parishioners initially resisted being vaccinated, so he vaccinated his immediate family and relatives to convince them it was harmless. When people saw that the epidemic passed by those the clergyman had vaccinated, opinions changed, and many subsequently allowed themselves to be vaccinated. See Bö, *Folkemedisin og lærd medisin,* 304–305, and Holck, "The Very Beginning," 33.

[15]The Kragerö minister Jacob Lund (1724–1785), for example, although he had studied medicine in Copenhagen in his youth, ultimately dedicated himself to theology instead. Yet he is said to have been the very first to give inoculations against smallpox in Norway. See Holck, "The Very Beginning," 33.

[16]Jens Juel (1580–1634), in order to entice Otto Sperling away from a post in Trondheim to accept the post of Chief Medical Officer in Oslo, asked, "What will you do in Trondheim? They have never had a physician there, nor do they know anything about medicine, but cure themselves with beer from Rostock and Lübeck, with mead and cloudberries when they have scurvy." But Sperling had few patients in Oslo as well and after only five years went back to his native Germany. As late as 1880, a doctor from Nordfjord records that only two out of 117 who had died in his district had been attended by a doctor during their last illness. See Holck, "The Very Beginning," 36.

[17]Möller, who was from Arendal and served as physician for the first Norwegian national assembly in Eidsvoll (1814), cited the parishioners' attitudes to explain why a doctor could not make a living, even as the only physician in a community of thirty or even forty thousand people. See Holck, "The Very Beginning," 32.

[18]Bö, *Folkemedisin og lærd medisin,* 30–33.

[19]Bö, *Folkemedisin og lærd medisin,* 27.

[20]Niels Hertzberg commented, "I marvel, though, that I never was arrested and sent to jail for *kvaksalveri* [quackery], *en uberettiget lege* [an unwarranted doctor], since for many years I had impersonated a physician." Bö, *Folkemedisin og lærd medisin,* 26. For mortals other than the minister, tradition paves the road to the Black Book with blasphemy, terror, and the eternal loss of one's soul: "If you want the Black Book, you must go to the church three Thursday evenings in a row. Each time you must walk three times counter-clockwise around the church, and after doing this the third evening, read the Lord's Prayer backwards. Then

the Evil One himself will appear with the Black Book in hand. But before you can take it, you must cut yourself in the finger and write your name in blood in another book the Evil One holds out. When this is done, you get the book. But once you have gotten it, you can never get rid of it again, and from that time on, you will belong to the devil." See Sigurd Nergaard, *Hulder og trollskap: Folkeminne fra Österdalen* (Oslo, 1925), 48.

The motif of differing outcomes for different users of the Black Book first emerged during the sixteenth- and seventeenth-century witch trials. Witches were burned for their magic, but ministers, despite being widely believed capable of the same feats—as evidenced by their possessing the Black Book—did not suffer the same fate. While witches were thought to be in service to the devil and thus to conduct black magic, ministers were viewed as the devil's overlord and, being so closely involved with sacred matters and having the Word in their power, were assumed to perform white magic rather than the black arts. See Andreas Seierstad, "Presten i norsk folketradisjon," in *Norvegia Sacra* 5 (1925), 15.

[21] Elisabeth Koren, *The Diary of Elisabeth Koren 1853–1855*, ed. and trans. David T. Nelson (Northfield, MN, 1955), 144.

[22] For diary entries including episodes of Elisabeth Koren being consulted for medical advice, see *The Diary of Elisabeth Koren*, 240, 253, 262, 263, 267, 295.

The view that it was part of the clergy's calling to relieve suffering of the sick was widespread during this period and, during the 1849 cholera epidemic in Chicago, *The Daily Democrat* (28 May 1849) reminded the clergy of their "duty to relieve the suffering of the poor and sick." Better able to fulfill this duty than most, the Swede Gustaf Unionius, ordained as an Episcopal priest in 1845, but who had previously studied medicine, converted a house in his Chicago neighborhood into a hospital to treat Swedish and Norwegian immigrants. See Odd S. Lovoll, *A Century of Urban Life: The Norwegians in Chicago before 1930* (Northfield, MN, 1988), 60–62.

[23] The comment occurs in Koren, *The Diary of Elisabeth Koren*, where she also writes: "To judge by what he [one of the parishioners] said, people believe we are skilled in medical matters" (295).

[24] Caja Munch, *The Strange American Way: The Letters of Caja Munch from Wiota, Wisconsin, 1855–1859* (Carbondale, IL, 1970), 65, 107.

[25] Joseph Shaw, *Bernt Julius Muus: Founder of St. Olaf College* (Northfield, MN, 1999), 260, 374, note 8. In Norway, too, the pastors' wives had

no doubt served alongside their husbands, to a far greater extent than history records, in meeting the parishioners' medical needs. Because the three immigrant women recorded in diaries and letters the totality of their encounter with America, history has not so readily lost track of them.

[26]Mrs. Assur H. Groth, then a girl of nineteen, made the journey with Clausen in the spring of 1853. She is quoted in Knut Gjerset and Ludvig Hektoen, "Health Conditions and the Practice of Medicine among the Early Norwegian Settlers 1825–1865," *Studies and Records* 1 (Northfield, MN, 1926), 11.

[27]Thalette Mathilde Brandt, "Some Social Aspects of Prairie Pioneering: The Reminiscences of a Pioneer Pastor's Wife," *Studies and Records* 7 (Northfield, MN, 1933), 6–7.

[28]Many additional examples could be cited of the fluidity of professions in the 1800s and early 1900s. According to Hjalmar Rued Holand, the Norwegian Moravian minister who founded the Norwegian settlement in Northern Door County was also the colony's only doctor. His parish stretched over many counties from Sturgeon Bay to Ephraim. After thirty-eight years of carrying out this double role, he took a course in medical school at the age of seventy-eight and began practice as a doctor in Sturgeon Bay. See *De norske settlementers historie: En oversigt over den norske indvandring til og bebyggelse af Amerikas nordvesten fra Amerikas opdagelse til indianerkrigen i nordvesten* (Ephraim, WI, 1908), 238–239. Dr. Ansgar Sommerfelt (b. 1864) of Kathryn, North Dakota, the son of a minister, studied at the University of Oslo, earned a degree in theology in 1889, and served as seamen's pastor in New York in 1890. Then in 1903 he fell sick with *nervesvækkelse ved overranstrengelse* [weakened nerves due to over-exertion] and remained ill for three years. During this time he became so interested in medical studies that he took medical training in Oslo and returned to America in 1913 to work as a doctor in Wisconsin and North Dakota. See Hans Astrup Jervell, *Nordmænd og norske hjem i Amerika* (Fargo, ND, [1916]), 179.

[29]N. E. Böe's inclination toward medicine had already surfaced during his student days at Augustana Seminary in 1866. In that year he volunteered to go into a month-long quarantine as the caregiver for five fellow students who had contracted smallpox.

A. Sophie Böe, *The Story of Father's Life,* unpublished typescript in the library of Luther Seminary in Saint Paul, Minnesota, adds that her father later delighted in reading popularized medical books, treating family members if they became ill, and stocking up on all kinds of home remedies to treat his parishioners (27). She further notes: "If he could help he always would—without charge, of course" (11).

³⁰Ronald Numbers and Judith Leavitt, eds., *Wisconsin Medicine: Historical Perspectives* (Madison, WI, 1981), 27.

³¹Wisconsin State Board of Health, *Seventh Annual Report, 1882*, 201, as quoted in Dale Treleven, "One Hundred Years of Health and Healing in Rural Wisconsin," in Numbers and Leavitt, *Wisconsin Medicine,* 138.

³²Laurence M. Larson, *The Log Book of a Young Immigrant* (Northfield, MN, 1939), 72. The importance of personality in healing is also attested by Leroy Davis in reminiscences of the 1870s diphtheria epidemic, which especially targeted children: "The physician's big job was to keep up the courage of the parents and cheer up his patients and perhaps incidentally, but most importantly of all, to keep up his own courage." See Leroy Davis, "Reminiscences," manuscript, Minnesota Historical Society, 79.

³³Hjalmar Rued Holand, *Coon Prairie: An Historical Report of the Norwegian Evangelical Lutheran Congregation at Coon Prairie Written on the Occasion of its 75th Anniversary in 1927,* trans. Oivind M. Hovde (Decorah, IA, 1977), 49–50.

³⁴O. S. Johnson, *Nybyggerhistorie fra Spring Grove og omegn* (Minneapolis, 1920), 227.

³⁵The reference occurs on page 36 of the novel, where the character is further described as having "the credulity that goes with ignorance" but also a "respect for book learning [that] was prodigious." Thor Helgeson included an account of a Black Book minister in the legends he recorded from his neighbors in Iola, Wisconsin. His account, however, concerns not a Norwegian-American Black Book minister, but the well-known cleric from Fåberg in Gudbrandsdal, Rasmus Lyng, about whom many Black Book legends circulated in Norway. "Pastor Lyng . . . had studied at the school of magic in Wittenberg and could read the Black Book backwards and forwards. If a student wished to become a pastor of any influence in olden times he had to matriculate in this school at Wittenberg and earn his degree there. The school always had twelve students. Upon graduation, eleven were permitted to leave, but the twelfth one Old Erik [the devil] kept as an assistant. The students

drew straws to see who was to become Erik's boy. At the time Pastor Lyng was getting his degree in the black arts, Lyng drew the shortest straw and was to serve as Erik's boy. But Lyng was . . . so learned and experienced in magic that he fooled Erik into taking his shadow instead." From Malcolm Rosholt, ed. and trans., *From the Indian Land: First-hand Account of Central Wisconsin's Pioneer Life* (Iola, WI, 1985), 257, translation slightly altered.

[36]O. K. Ödegard, *Valdrespresta* (Kristiania, 1917), 29–31.

[37]The account continues with more evidence of strained relations between the Valdres minister and the community: "Ola Haadestad [one of the cotters] had once said something to the effect that the devil could come and take this minister. Ruge found out about this, since a minister has almost as many ears as a king. And once when Ole Hakkestad met the minister up on the Slire hill, the minister said, 'As you can see, the devil hasn't taken me so far, my dear Ole.' 'It's not too late yet,' Ole replied and abruptly took his leave." From Ödegard, *Valdrespresta,* 29–31.

[38]Caja Munch, *The Strange American Way,* 30.

[39]The letter writer continues, "That there has been unrest in religious matters here is another matter which in no way contradicts this." And further: "Anyone can understand how much easier it is for a troubled soul to confess to an open and mild man. I can testify from personal experience that it is very difficult for a person troubled by sin to open his heart to a [Norwegian] pastor. He is regarded as a haunting spirit, if not worse. People scare children by saying that the pastor will come and take them away. It is regrettable that people should be so estranged from their pastors. I mean this in general, but there are always exceptions." The letter was originally printed in *Agder,* 21 February 1879. Translation from Frederick Hale, ed. and trans., *Their Own Saga* (Minneapolis, 1986), 128–129.

An Immigrant Preacher and His Sermons: A Case Study in Norwegian-American Lutheran Preaching

Øyvind T. Gulliksen

PREACHING IS EMINENTLY an oral skill. When the Norwegian-American culture flourished in the Midwest a hundred years ago, pastors delivered sermons by the thousands and people by the hundreds of thousands heard them every week. This particular kind of American sermon, preached and listened to in the Norwegian language, has long since vanished, only to be revived on certain commemorative occasions. We do not know much about how these sermons were delivered and heard, but we are able to assess the written form of at least some of them. Some were published in American church papers and periodicals.[1] Many were published in volumes of sermons for the liturgical year, and a few of the most influential Norwegian-American church leaders, like Ulrik Vilhelm Koren, had whole collections of sermons published.[2] Here, however, I want to take as a case study the unpublished sermons of a pastor of the Norwegian Synod who served congregations in rural Wisconsin at the end of the nineteenth century and the beginning of the twentieth century, Søren Sørensen Urberg (1861–1930).[3]

Sermons constitute an important genre of American literature, and we must consider the Norwegian-American sermon as an *American* text. American sermons address a wide variety of themes ranging from the spiritual verities of Jonathan Edwards's "Sinners in the Hands of an Angry God" to the social concerns so prominent in the sermons of Martin Luther King, Jr. We have anthologies of Puritan sermons, of African-American sermons, of American sermons in general, but American immigrant sermons are harder to find in print.[4] Historians of ethnic church history and scholars of immigrant literature have clearly not regarded the body of American sermons in Scandinavian languages to be of much interest. In their standard study, *The Lutheran Church among Norwegian-Americans,* for example, E. Clifford Nelson and Eugene Fevold pay far more attention to congregational meetings and institutional structures than to the liturgical practice and preaching in ordinary congregations.[5] While such sermons may seem wearisomely ordinary to the contemporary reader, they nevertheless reflect an important literary genre and constituted a central form of symbolic expression for this immigrant community. Often read, and even more often heard, these sermons were occasions for reflection on the part of a good many people.

A number of questions arise when we consider *American* sermons preached in languages like Norwegian, Swedish, German, or Finnish. Did immigrant pastors choose topics and themes, the rhetoric, or the styles of famous American sermons rendered in English? Did immigrant groups in the United States listen to sermons given in their own mother tongue, but which introduced patterns established by earlier Puritan or later mainstream American preachers? To what extent were immigrant sermons inspired by American theology? What sort of modifications did the prevailing Lutheran orthodoxy in sermons of immigrant pastors undergo as a consequence of the reorganization of their own church life in the United States? Did preachers educated in the old countries adhere to their traditional homiletics when they preached in the new country? To what extent did pastors and congregations feel that the preaching of the gospel was tied to the language of the old country? Was their American immigrant experience reflected at all in the sermons? If we, as modern readers, are willing to suspend our preconceived notions of answers to these and similar questions, we may gain insight into how such sermons reflect an intriguing double consciousness in both speaker and hearer in an immigrant culture. While we cannot yet answer all of these questions, we can consider at least some of them on the basis of this case study.

A study of American sermons given in Norwegian will indicate that the purpose of these sermons was to ensure the proclamation of the gospel and the proper administration of the sacraments in the immigrant community and to do so by retaining the Norwegian language, at least during the early period of Norwegian-American history. In that sense the sermon was typically written to preserve something rather than to entice the listener into new territories. Immigrant members of the congregation expected to have Scripture explained and applied to their lives in the *new* country in the language of the *old,* the language in which they had first learned their Bible stories and catechism. Did this linguistic policy make immigrant homilies less innovative and less creative than other American sermons?

The typical listeners to Norwegian-American sermons around 1900 were farmers and their children; they were immigrants or the descendants of immigrants. The older of these had quite realistic notions of what it meant to be migrants, a metaphor commonly used in preaching and often found in stories of the Old Testament. In this matter they were more experienced than their kinfolk who had remained in Norway. With this in mind, we might well wonder if Norwegian-American pastors often applied the metaphor of the "migrant" in their explication and application of the biblical texts. How often did references to the old country occur in their sermons? What were the purposes of such references and how long did they make sense to the congregations? Did the image of the old country appear in sermons as a reassuring ideal or in negative contrast to the new country? How did immigrant pastors apply the central biblical metaphors of "journeying" and "homecoming"? It is not surprising that a recent volume on the special status of American homiletics is entitled *Cadences of Home: Preaching among Exiles,* and that its author returns to this question, which is as old as the exile of the Israelites in Babylon. He asks us to "consider what happens if we reread our own journey to this time and place in light of that biblical narrative."[6] Were such questions asked in American immigrant sermons of the late nineteenth century? We know that when Ole E. Rølvaag's minister enters the Norwegian settlement in *Giants in the Earth,* he applies these images to his preaching of the gospel, much to the satisfaction of his listeners.[7] But were immigrant experience and immigrant theology actually combined in the Norwegian-American preaching of this era?

With such questions in mind I have turned to the sermons of a pastor of the Norwegian Synod who preached to the same congregations for more than thirty-five years in rural Wisconsin, in the town of Blair and the surrounding area, from the early 1890s until he died in 1930. Emigrating from Norway as a young man, Søren Sørensen Urberg (1861–1930) was trained as a pastor in the Midwest. He left an astonishing number of sermons, a brief diary from his final year at the seminary, and several letters. Over the years, he received tempting calls to move from the congregation he served in Blair, but as he wrote in a letter of 1903, "A friend of mine has just been to Chicago where he was robbed for all he had on the open street. I am staying in Blair."[8]

It is difficult to estimate how much the teaching of homiletics at the Synod seminary during the early 1890s was inspired by contemporary American debate on preaching. Since the 1850s influential pastors such as Henry Ward Beecher (1813–1887) had emphasized that the actual experience of preaching rather than classical rhetoric was the key to homiletics, but Beecher's liberal, evangelical sermons may not have found their way to the bookshelves of many Norwegian-American pastors at the time.[9] At this point, they were more likely to acquire books published by leading theological figures in Norway or German Lutherans in the United States. Indeed, in the early 1890s, the Norwegian Synod seminary at Robbinsdale was undoubtedly less receptive to homiletic trends from Norway or New England than to pastoral theology taught according to the standards of the conservative Missouri Synod, which continued to influence the teaching of theology within the Norwegian Synod even after students who were aiming for the ministry in Norwegian Synod congregations no longer had to study at the Missouri Synod seminary in St. Louis, Missouri.[10] In a diary Urberg wrote just before his final examinations at Robbinsdale, he complains that he has memorized the doctrine of original sin until, as he writes, "I am blue in the face."[11] The opportunity to enter into the work of ministry in Wisconsin must have come as something of a relief after years of study at the seminary.

Urberg's call in Wisconsin consisted of three Norwegian-American Lutheran rural congregations: Trempealeau Valley, Blair, and North Beaver Creek. During his ministry he added new churches at Pine Creek (1894) and Ettrick (1898) to his charge. He must have considered preaching essential to his task as a pastor, because when he had been in the call for about thirty years he felt a need to make a detailed account of his sermons. After a meticulous survey he concluded that he had at the time delivered "3114 sermons" in Blair and the community roundabout.[12] Urberg was a conscientious writer and custodian of his own sermons, many of which he kept in a personal file. After he died, a box full of these hand-written sermons was given to one of his sons, also a pastor. All in all, this precious box contains roughly 500 of Urberg's sermons. In time they range from the mid 1890s to shortly before he died in 1930. They were categorized either chronologically for the whole church year, centering on Christmas and Easter, or they were filed under special events. They include confirmation sermons, Thanksgiving sermons, sermons on missionary service, one ordination sermon, and several wedding and funeral sermons. Almost all of these American sermons, except for a handful he wrote in English for young people in the congregation towards the end of his life, were written in Norwegian.[13]

During the time of Søren Urberg's ministry, Norwegian immigrants and their descendants made up a large percentage of people in Blair and the adjacent areas. Pioneer Norwegian farmers first came to this place in the 1850s, most of them from other parts of Wisconsin, and Norwegian-American settlers had already lived in this area for forty years when Urberg began his ministry. As late as 1916 the number of Norwegian-American church buildings in Trempealeau County was estimated to be more than twenty.[14] This was in part a consequence of the election controversy of the 1880s, the so-called *nådevalgsstriden* [election controversy].[15] This strife, in fact, had severe consequences for the Norwegian Synod congregation in Blair and the surrounding communities. By the time Urberg arrived, the Norwegian Synod church in Blair, which had been the largest congregation of Norwegian Americans in the town, was torn asunder and reduced to the status of a minority church within the community. Most of its former members had joined the newly formed United Church. Urberg, however, remained faithful to the Norwegian Synod to the end of its existence, that is, until the merger of 1917, of which he was strongly in favor. The bitter struggles of the 1880s are not much reflected in Urberg's sermons.[16] He must have decided to let that remain a thing of the past. When he was referred to in the North Beaver Creek congregation as "the Synod pastor with a Haugean heart," he took this as a fine compliment.[17] That may be an indication that Lutheran orthodoxy and nineteenth-century evangelical pietism were often harmonized in sermons such as Urberg's. In fact, the identical compliment was repeated in Urberg's obituary in *The Lutheran Church Herald*: "His ideal was to combine in life and preaching the old Synod's conservatism in doctrine and practice with the old Haugianer heart-religion."[18] This is an interesting Norwegian-American brand of combining the objective and the subjective, realism and romanticism, reason and emotion.[19]

When Urberg started to preach in the Synod churches of Trempealeau Valley, the religious map of the valley had for the first time become truly American. Nearly up until his entry upon the scene in 1893, the Synod had gathered the majority of the Norwegian Americans in the community into its congregations. In other words, the ethnic and religious identity of Norwegian-American society had been practically the same and not fundamentally unlike that of a rural parish in Norway. From the early 1890s on, however, the Synod pastor had to face an American pluralistic congregational life; he had to reckon with American denominationalism even among the Norwegian-speaking Americans in the valley. Often when Urberg refers to "our people" as "*vaart folk*," a term Norwegians of the old country would have taken to refer to any Norwegian, the term does not even include all Norwegian immigrants and their descendants in the Blair community; this phrase is often restricted to those who had become and remained members of the Norwegian Synod. It is important to have this aspect of American church history in mind when we look at Urberg's sermons.

Although the local influence of Urberg as pastor of the Norwegian Synod congregation may have been reduced after the election controversy, he had wide cultural interests. For years he was the chairman of the Telemark *bygdelag* in Wisconsin, a society of immigrants coming from the area of Telemark in Norway. He wrote speeches on the dramas of Henrik Ibsen and on the poetry of Aasmund Olavson Vinje, both of whom he highly respected. In the Blair parsonage people met not only for Bible study; the pastor also led a reading society that met regularly to discuss texts by Norwegian writers such as Vinje, Ibsen, Bjørnson, and Garborg.[20] Urberg was a friend of the Norwegian-American writers Jon Norstog and Waldemar Ager. When Urberg died in 1930, Ager wrote an obituary in *Reform*.[21] Like Ager, Urberg thought that Norwegian ought to continue in use as an American language, in both oral and written forms. For him, at least, his sermons had a double purpose: both to keep his listeners in a life of faith and also to keep the flock using the language of the old country, with Norwegian as their true American language. Here Urberg, the pastor, and Ager, the author, shared common interests. In fact, the alliance with a cultural figure and author like Waldemar Ager may have meant just as much to Urberg as his contact with the leadership of the Synod. Even though Urberg may have shared the Synod's skepticism toward the "Anti-Missourians," he could very well, in his preaching, adopt aspects of Haugean pietism or even the rhetoric of Grundtvig.[22] Historians of Norwegian-American church life should not always assume that the doctrinal struggles that were of ultimate concern among the leaders of the various synods were just as strictly adhered to by pastors on the local level. Urberg's immigrant homiletics, in fact, must be linked to a broader cultural outlook. At the fiftieth anniversary for the congregation in North Beaver Creek in 1909, Urberg had the congregation sing, in Norwegian, Grundtvig's famous hymn "*Guds ord det er vort arvegods det vore barn skal være. Gud giv oss i vår grav den ros, Vi holdt det høit I ære. . . .*"[23] Grundtvig's theology may have been indigestible to a good many Norwegian-American church leaders at this time and earlier, but his hymns were used, as by Urberg in North Beaver Creek, both to strengthen the faith of churchgoers *and* to remind them of their Danish-Norwegian cultural heritage.

Given the pastor's interest in the contemporary literature of his day, one would expect that he would use examples from literature to support his points in sermons, but references to his favorite authors are practically nonexistent in his sermons. An analysis of his sermons for Easter, on the other hand, will make clear that all the ingredients of Lutheran orthodoxy are there. The American liberal theology of his day does not enter his sermons, not even as a school of thought to be countered. On the other hand, a classical Protestant theology of the atonement, an emphasis on the resurrection as proof of life after death, the idea of God's inscrutable and indisputable will are all there. His Easter meditations on the suffering of Christ are rendered in painful detail and given in the present tense, such as "then parts of his skin fall away and his Holy blood drips on the ground." Apparently Urberg never felt the need to clarify the paradox of the divine necessity of the crucifixion and the fact that it was caused and provoked by a mindless mob, because for him the application of the Good Friday text is clear: "each one of us was present. . . . Our sins were the cords in the whip that flogged him. . . . We were all there" in Jerusalem when it happened.[24]

When he preached, Urberg would sometimes refer to the double consciousness of the immigrant. The older listeners in his congregation had two frames of reference, an old country and a new country. In a Good Friday sermon he compares Golgotha to "a small-town American courthouse square." But when Christ is mocked by the mob along the way the comparison is to "running the gauntlet in Norway a hundred years ago."[25] Urberg also explains to his congregation that church practices were carried with immigrants to the Midwest. "In the land of our fathers the fourth Friday after Easter was declared by royal decree to be a day of prayer and repentance [*bots- og bededag*], a custom we have taken with us to this country."[26] On the other hand, when in 1894 he asks for "forgiveness for our sins, the sins of our fellow countrymen and the sins of our country," he refers to the United States.[27]

A few sermons categorized as "Thanksgiving sermons" from 1895 to 1923 reveal a rural Midwestern setting. When, in the fall of 1899, the pastor addresses a congregation of Trempealeau Valley farmers, he says, "we asked God to bless the growth of our fields and God has listened to our prayers and we received a blessed harvest this year. Today we will gather in gratitude to celebrate the rich gifts he has bestowed on us, praising him for giving us bread." This sermon is clearly a continuation of the Norwegian-Danish *takksigelses dag* [day of thanksgiving] transferred to the Midwest and conflated with the American Thanksgiving Day, another interesting double context for the immigrant pastor. References to the civil character of Thanksgiving Day, however, are entirely absent.[28]

Urberg must have been convinced that his sermons did not lose their sap over the years and that they could be repeated with small alterations. In all likelihood, Urberg never read the neo-orthodox theology of Karl Barth, but he seems to have preached in a way that much accorded with the ideas of Barth. Urberg rarely applied stories from outside the Bible and he must have insisted that sermons be written, just as Barth was later to do: "A sermon is a speech which we have prepared word for word and written down. This alone accords with its dignity."[29] In a sermon given in 1894 on Acts 24:24–27, the story of Felix and his wife listening to Paul, Urberg says that "a sermon is delivered, not to make us satisfied with the preacher, but to make us dissatisfied with ourselves." His sentence could have been taken verbatim out of Barth.[30] These sermons were clearly not written to entertain, but to proclaim.

Urberg's funeral sermons are of particular interest, because here the pastor has to be specific. We expect that he will at least offer a few sentences concerning the life story of the deceased and offer special support to the bereaved. Some thirty of his funeral sermons were kept in the box I received. In addition, I have also found eleven funeral sermons by Urberg in the archives at Luther Seminary in Saint Paul, Minnesota. Nearly all of these funeral sermons were written in Norwegian. Some are sermons he would use again and again, for instance a sermon for the burial of children and a sermon for the deceased young mother. A few are written for special people and used only once, such as his long funeral sermon for Knut K. Hagestad, who for many years had been a leading figure in the congregation in Beaver Creek. The necrology from this sermon was published in *Skandinaven*.[31]

Most of his funeral sermons were meditations on biblical texts and could therefore be used several times. One of these, for example, is based on Hebrews 4:9-11. This handwritten sermon consists of seven short pages. At the end Urberg has kept a written record of when, where, and for whom this particular sermon was preached. It was first delivered in Trempealeau Valley Church in 1907 to commemorate Kari Sylfest, repeated in Blair in 1908, in Ettrick in 1918, in Taylor in 1922, in Fagernes Church in 1925, in Tamarack in 1929, and finally in Blair in August of 1930, shortly before Urberg himself died.

This particular funeral sermon must have been intended to commemorate the death of women. Only two or three men are listed for whom this sermon was used. The rest are women with Norwegian names: Tone Herreid, Sarah Olsen Storlie, Lina Ødegaard, Julia Ekern, and so on. Why this sermon was particularly well suited to immigrant women is difficult to say. The text from the letter to the Hebrews seems neutral as to gender: "So then, there remains a Sabbath rest for the people of God; for whosoever enters God's rest also ceases from his labors as God did from his." To the pastor, the idea of a Sabbath rest may have been particularly applicable to women who had worked on Wisconsin farms their whole adult lives. Notice also that the idea of being a pilgrim and a mother is combined, "We celebrate because the tired pilgrim at last has arrived. We grieve over her who was a mother for us all." Life is seen in this sermon as a pilgrim's journey; the heavenly rest comes at the end of a long "pilgrimage," sometimes tied to the history of the person's immigration: "And it is our hope that this old woman has come to this Sabbath rest for the people of God. Born, baptized over there among the mountains of Norway, she was instructed in the Lutheran faith in her childhood, a faith that was affirmed by her Confirmation and in which she remained. Nothing could take her away from the church of her fathers, her great sacred heritage."[32]

Here and elsewhere the double identity of the immigrant is clear. In another funeral sermon life is regarded by the pastor as "a constant migration" [*en stadig vandring*]. The text for this sermon is Hebrews 13:14, "For here we have no lasting city, but we seek the city which is to come." Urberg explains the use of the verse this way, "The first part of today's text voices a truth that no one can deny: we have no lasting city." It is as if the life of the deceased proves this statement, because Urberg goes on to say, "Born, baptized, brought up and confirmed on the Scandinavian peninsula, he found no permanent place there, but guided by God, he emigrated over the vast sea to a new place on the vast territories of the west, but not even here did he get a firm footing but had to lay down his tired bones at his last resting place, trading his changing route for an everlasting life."[33] Urberg then goes on to make this life story of the deceased immigrant a metaphor for life in general: "Let this death inscribe the serious words in our hearts: we have no lasting city."

Here the real life story of the Norwegian immigrant is tied to a religious idea and finally to a verse from Hebrews, as if the life of the immigrant is particularly valid and appropriate for the use of the New Testament passage. Then Urberg interestingly applies the story and the New Testament verse to the inescapability of death: "And is not this the case with all people. Who among the many millions who call this earth their home has remained here and thereby could challenge the truth of the word of God we have just read?" The image of having no abiding city covers us all; as "wandering pilgrims" we must seek "the heavenly home."[34] To underscore the point that all those attending the funeral were included in the category of pilgrims, Urberg explains that the deceased in this case "was baptized in the name of the Triune God. In baptism he became a child of God"; that he later repeated his baptismal promise, but that God had given him a small portion [*et åndeligt*(?) *lidet pund*]. By this rather straightforward addition, Urberg may have meant that in spite of the fact that the deceased's capacities in this case were small and "his comprehension was limited," he was not to be pushed aside: "Where little is given, little will be demanded."[35]

In a funeral sermon of 1897 for a member who had fought for Lincoln's cause during the Civil War, Urberg tells that "for years he had a poor body, which he had gotten while he was defending his 'adopted country'" [*adoptivland*]. Urberg refers to the American Civil War in his sermon as a fight against the evil of slavery. He is not bound by the earlier, rather unclear position on the Civil War taken by leading figures of the Norwegian Synod. Says Urberg: "Years ago, when loose elements [*løse element*] did not want to adhere to the laws of the land, when it was decided that our black brothers should not be treated as cattle any more, because it was a blot of shame [*en skamplett*] on American freedom, then he set out, sword in hand, to restore the laws of the land at the risk of losing his own life." The text for this funeral sermon is, interestingly enough, from Genesis 49:33, when Jacob, after blessing his children, "drew up his feet into the bed, and breathed his last, and was gathered to his people." Now this one-time American soldier has "like Jacob breathed his last and been gathered up to his people."[36]

Sermons given at funerals for children and young parents bring a keen sense of the precariousness of life in the community. One such sermon uses Mark 14:36 from the Easter story as words of comfort to a family stricken by the sudden death of a mother, "Father, all things are possible to Thee; remove this cup from me; yet not what I will, but what thou wilt." "There are," Urberg admits, "some deaths which will move a stone heart. We see in our midst a young, sad widower whom God had given a faithful, diligent, and good wife.... We see six children, of whom two or three cannot yet realize the loss.... She was irreplaceable for husband and children, but no art of medicine could keep the wife and mother alive."[37]

Funeral sermons for the old may have been less tragic, although Urberg must have felt that a whole ethnic culture was dying out with the old-timers in the congregation. In 1897 he chose a verse from I Thessalonians to comfort the people present: "But we would not have you ignorant, brethren, concerning those who are asleep, that you may not grieve as others do who have no hope" (4:13). This service was conducted for a pioneer among Norwegian-American farmers in the district, one "who 43 years ago came here to what was then a wild and desolate valley . . . he took part in the founding of the Synod congregation here 40 years ago this May and he has since been a member."[38] In a funeral sermon of 1909, Urberg feels the need to thank the deceased for his steadfastness through the church struggles in the Norwegian-American churches some thirty years earlier. Holding fast to the essentials of the faith of childhood here undoubtedly means loyalty to the Norwegian Synod: "Thank you for your firm standing in your childhood faith during the several storms raging within our churches."[39]

As a pastor in one rural area for so long, Urberg likely knew every single member of his congregation. Like a parish pastor in Norway, he felt a responsibility for most Norwegian Americans in the community, even if the members of his congregation were those who had been baptized in the Lutheran faith and "who turn to and renew the covenant with God." Not all of them did, even if they were baptized as children. Occasionally, his funeral sermons will emphasize the need of conversion. He says about one member of his congregation, "one of the suffering men in this valley": "Thank God that he was given time for a complete conversion [*en grundig omvendelse*]. Oh, how many times over the last few years did we talk together about sin and grace. And even long after God had given him the full assurance that he was a pardoned sinner and that all his transgressions were concealed, up to the very last moments he could weep the tears of gratitude because his sins had been removed."[40] This is important evidence that, contrary to historical stereotype, not only the clergy of Hauge's Synod but pastors of the Norwegian Synod as well were wont to speak of conversion in their sermons.

In immigrant letters home to family and friends in Norway, heaven is often described as a place where there is no more parting. In several of Urberg's sermons the idea of heaven is expressed in similar ways. In heaven there is *"aldrig er skilsmisse mere"* ["nevermore any parting"], a commonplace that is echoed in hundreds of immigrant letters to people back home in Norway. It is not difficult to imagine why, to the immigrant members of the congregation, parting from relatives was hell and joining hands was heaven.

In between the pages of one funeral sermon, Urberg kept a note clearly written by the husband of the deceased in order to thank family and friends for tending to his wife before she died. It was quite common that a family member would write a few words on a note and have them read by the minister. It may be that Urberg read it for the husband and then kept the note. It is written in a somewhat irregular Norwegian, with a spelling that is not standard: *"Je vil sige eder jertelig tak for eders Sympati med mig og min kone under hendes Sygdom"* ["I would like to say a cordial thank you for your sympathy to me and my wife during her illness"]. He explains that several women had come to tend to his wife before she died, and he uses the Norwegian-American expression *"at tænde til henne"* ["to tend to her"] and then lists the names of the people who have helped and—with a matter-of-factness that may have produced unexpected reactions—the number of weeks they had been there: "Berta Nielsen 14 weeks, Agnes Quammen 11 weeks, Esther Lekve 7 weeks, and Berta Anderson, one week."[41]

In the Trempealeau Valley Church in 1927, Urberg took Psalm 17:15 as his text for a funeral sermon: "As for me, I shall behold thy face in righteousness; when I awake, I shall be satisfied with beholding thy form." This psalm may not necessarily concern the idea of everlasting life, but it is used here as if it were from the New Testament. Urberg begins this sermon with a summary of the life of Isaac, whom he refers to as a patriarch, and who is buried by his sons. About Isaac, Urberg says that he did not accomplish as much as his father, Abraham, but that "he lived a more quiet and secluded life, a witness to God who cultivated the fields, but who, like all pilgrims, got worn out, and at the end the angel of death entered and called him to life everlasting." This story about Isaac is then interestingly used as a model for the immigrant Urberg is burying in Wisconsin. The next sentence reads, "The old grandfather whose earthly remains we will bury today was also gathered to his people, an old man and full of years," the expression used in the Old Testament for the death of Isaac and Abraham. Here the life of a Wisconsin immigrant may be read as an analog to the life of a patriarch of the Old Testament. Like the patriarch of old, the immigrant, according to the pastor, was "blessed with a strong body and good health. In addition, he had added unto him twenty years more than the seventy that Moses says are the years of dust. Like a worthy old patriarch he walked among us and now is gathered to his people in a quiet and peaceful death." He goes on to say that in his younger and more powerful days the deceased was a thrifty man and successful in his earthly calling. He nevertheless "followed the advice of King David, do not lose your heart to earthly possessions. . . . The Bible and the hymnbook were his daily reading and the older he got, the more he loved those books. This is the right way. God grant that we may choose to walk the same way."[42]

In his sermons for the burial of children the pastor asks the most obvious question: How could this happen? The framework of these sermons was often the same, even if he refers in a few sentences to the brief life of the child and the situation of the grieving family. A typical example is a funeral sermon he preached for a child of one Andrew Quammen at Beaver Creek. The same sermon is repeated over the years eight times with the names of the children listed at the end: the child of Otto Lie, Emil Granberg, Bert Erikson, Gustav Skogstad, and so on. Everything is couched in terms of the pastor's theology. This text is from John 13:7 where Jesus explains why he washes the feet of his disciples: "Jesus answered him, 'What I am doing you do not know now, but afterward you will understand.'" Urberg takes this sentence out of its New Testament context and uses it to reassure his listeners of life everlasting. "Why did the Lord do this now? What I am doing now you do not know. A year and a half ago God gave you a child. Now he has taken it back. Why has God done that? Concerning the child we have a firm answer: in baptism he declared her to be his adopted child and grafted into Christ and now he has taken her soul out of all dangers so that it will not be lost. You have a child in heaven." Urberg's answer in these sermons is always that God is omnipotent. This sometime leads him to the verge of fatalism. God's will is done and he does what he does to save some of us from later dangers in life: "God's plan is always best."[43]

The reference to God's plan as best had also been offered several times as a conclusive and undebatable remark in favor of personal decisions to emigrate from Norway. For more than thirty years, Urberg preached among Norwegian immigrants in rural Wisconsin who had made this very decision. He knew his congregations well and was himself an immigrant. Even though Urberg's sermons were given in Norwegian, they must be evaluated as representing an American genre. The homiletics of the old country could not be adhered to even if the pastor may have wanted to do so, simply because his congregation had undergone a different experience. The sermons of a Synod pastor in Wisconsin may lead us to reflect not only on the orthodox-pietist spirit of the man who wrote them. They ask us as well to reconsider the complicated and strikingly double horizon of the immigrant who listened to them. These Norwegian-American sermons thus reflect a double context, shaped by the traditions of preaching in the old country, modulated by experience in the new.

NOTES

[1]Sermons were published regularly in periodicals of all the major Norwegian-American synods, such as *Budbæreren* issued by Hauge's Synod; *Kirkelig Maanedstidende* and *Evangelisk Luthersk Kirketidende,* published by the Norwegian Synod; and in *Lutheraneren* published by the Conference for the Norwegian-Danish Evangelical Lutheran Church in America and later by the United Norwegian Lutheran Church in America.

[2]An example of a relatively early collection in Norwegian by pastors of the Norwegian Synod is Einar Wulfsberg, ed., *Prædikener over Kirke-Aarets Evangelier holdte af Prester i den norske Synode i Amerika* (Decorah, IA, 1888). An example of a later collection of sermons in English by pastors of the United Norwegian Lutheran Church is O. M. Norlie, ed., *A Free Text Church Postil by Pastors of the United Norwegian Lutheran Church of America* (Minneapolis, 1913). Koren's sermons appear in vol. 1 of *Samlede Skrifter af Dr. theol. V. Koren,* ed. Paul Koren, 4 vols. (Decorah, IA, 1912).

[3]Born into a relatively poor family on the Southern coast of Norway in 1861, Søren Sørensen Urberg was not recruited to the clergy on the basis of family tradition. His father died before the boy was born, and when his mother remarried they moved to the southern part of Telemark, where he grew up and was confirmed in the state church of Norway in 1877. He went to Viggo Ullmann's folk high school and completed his preparatory exam for the University in Oslo in 1887. He

started to study theology in Norway, but meager resources kept him from further studies and in 1889 he emigrated to the United States, settling first in Glendorado, Minnesota, where he worked as a farm hand. He desired to enter the ministry and in 1890 he was enrolled as a student at the seminary of the Norwegian Synod then located in Robbinsdale, outside of Minneapolis. Here Urberg took his examinations in 1893, after four years of study. His teachers were Professors H. G. Stub, Johannes T. Ylvisaker, and J. B. Frich. Even before he had his degree in theology, he had been called to serve as the pastor in Blair, Wisconsin. For a biographical study of Søren S. Urberg, see my *En synodeprest blir teksthistorie: Søren S. Urberg i Wisconsin, 1893–1930* (Bø i Telemark, 1991). Sketches of Urberg's life as a pastor are also given in *"One in the Spirit": 125th Anniversary 1859–1984, North Beaver Creek Lutheran Church* (Columbia, SC, 1984), 25–30, and in *First Lutheran Church, Blair, Wisconsin: Centennial 1879–1979* (Blair, WI, 1979), 8.

[4]The Library of America has published a comprehensive anthology of American sermons entitled *American Sermons: The Pilgrims to Martin Luther King,* ed. Michael Warner (New York, 1999). A collection of sermons written by African-American pastors is *Best Black Sermons,* ed. William M. Philpot (Valley Forge, PA, 1972).

[5]E. Clifford Nelson and Eugene L. Fevold, *The Lutheran Church among Norwegian-Americans: A History of the Evangelical Lutheran Church,* 2 vols. (Minneapolis, 1960).

[6]Walter Brueggemann, *Cadences of Home: Preaching among Exiles* (Louisville, KY, 1997), 112. I am interested in the rhetoric used by Brueggemann here, not his arguments.

[7]In fact, the preaching of Rølvaag's minister on the Dakota prairies in *Giants in the Earth* comes very close to the homiletic practice of seventeenth-century American Puritans. Rølvaag has his immigrant community gather around the minister to listen to a sermon in which their situation is linked to that of the Israelites of the Old Testament: "The minister preached on the coming of the Israelites into the Land of Canaan. He began by reminding his hearers of the dangers which the Children of Israel had been obliged to pass through, and of the struggles and tribulations which they had been forced to endure. He set forth what had been promised them if they would remain faithful to the heritage of their fathers and obedient to the law which the Lord had given

them as their guide. . . . Then the minister shifted the scene, applying the parable to those who stood before him; they, too, had wandered in search of a Land of Canaan; from the ancient home of their race they had fared forth, far away over the ocean into a foreign country; here they had settled now, here they proposed to strike root again; and here their seed would multiply from generation to generation, ages without end" (Ole E. Rølvaag, *Giants in the Earth* [New York, 1991 (1927)], 362). This sermon by Rølvaag's Norwegian-American pastor uses Old Testament references in much the same way as did John Winthrop in 1630. The passage may indeed have been inspired by American parallels and cannot be read as an allegedly accurate rendering of a typical Norwegian-American sermon of the 1870s.

[8]The letter is dated 28 October 1903. Quoted in my study *En synode-prest blir teksthistorie*, 4.

[9]At the height of his career Henry Ward Beecher was undoubtedly one of the most popular preachers in Victorian America. His *Yale Lectures on Preaching* (New York, 1872) was reissued several times in the subsequent decades.

[10]"The Norwegian Synod developed a deep affection for the Missouri Synod, which since its organization in 1847, had brought a strong confessional reaction into American Lutheranism." Nelson and Fevold, *The Lutheran Church among Norwegian-Americans*, 1:161. Even after the Norwegian Synod established its own seminary, the doctrinal stance of the Missouri Synod continued to exert a powerful influence among the ordinands of the Norwegian Synod.

[11]Urberg has entitled his diary "*Smånotiser af Søren S. Urberg, begyndt 30. marts [18]93, bestemt for mig selv sam[t] mine nærmeste.*" Urberg's complaint on dogmatics is from an entry of 19 April 1893. A copy of Urberg's short diary from his last year at the seminary in Robbinsdale was given to me by his daughter, Fernanda Malmin, in Minneapolis, in 1983.

[12]Quoted in Gulliksen, *En synodeprest blir teksthistorie*, 5.

[13]The box belonged to Søren's youngest son, Sigurd Urberg, himself a minister, of Waterville, Minnesota. In 1997 the box was cordially handed over to me to facilitate my studies of Urberg's sermons. It is temporarily stored in my office at Telemark University College. In this essay sermons from this collection will be referred to as "Urberg file."

[14]Ann Legreid, "Through Years of Turbulence, Years of Calm: A History of the North Beaver Creek Congregations," in *"One in the Spirit,"* 29.

[15]For a brief discussion of this controversy locating it in the context of American Lutheran history as a whole, see Eugene L. Fevold, "Coming of Age, 1875-1900," in *The Lutherans in North America*, ed. E. Clifford Nelson (Minneapolis, 1975), 313-325.

[16]Ann Legreid has written extensively on the religious schisms of the 1880s as they affected the congregations in Blair and North Beaver Creek prior to Urberg's coming. See her essay, "Community Building, Conflict, and Change: Geographic Perspectives on the Norwegian-American Experience in Frontier Wisconsin," in *Wisconsin: Land and Life*, ed. Robert C. Ostergren and Thomas R. Vale (Madison, WI, 1997), 300-319.

[17]Information given in Ann Legreid, "Through Years of Turbulence," 25.

[18]*The Lutheran Church Herald*, 14 October 1930.

[19]Gerhard O. Forde has argued that Old Synod pastors "sought their refuge in the objective scriptural witness" and that their "joy was a kind of calm confidence, not a quixotic emotionalism." See his essay "The 'Old Synod': A Search for Objectivity," in *Striving for Ministry: Centennial Essays Interpreting the Heritage of Luther Theological Seminary*, ed. Warren A. Quanbeck et al. (Minnneapolis, 1977). Leigh D. Jordahl has also emphasized the coming together of reason and emotion among the pastors of the Norwegian Synod. They had, according to Jordahl, "a dream of order, culture, orthodox faith, and a vital piety joined together—the Synod was an interesting experiment of merging faith and culture in such a way as to produce noble service." See "The Gentry Tradition—Men and Women of a Leadership Class," in *Church Roots: Stories of Nine Immigrant Groups That Became The American Lutheran Church*, ed. Charles P. Lutz (Minneapolis, 1985), 116.

[20]A list of books in Søren S. Urberg's library shows that he owned the collected works of Arne Garborg, Aasmund O. Vinje, and Alexander Kielland, as well as an edition of Ibsen's letters. The list was provided to me by Urberg's daugher, Fernanda Malmin, Minneapolis, in a letter in 1984.

[21]"A steadfast friend of all things Norwegian, a warm-hearted, an always understanding and serious pastor—dependable and considerate,

as a father to all. And now he too has laid down his pilgrim staff. But, blessing will grow following such a man's work." Thus wrote Waldemar Ager about Søren S. Urberg in *Reform,* 2 October 1930.

Søren's son, Sigurd, writes in a letter that his father conversed with Norwegian-American authors such as Waldemar Ager and Jon Norstog, as well as "with the farm worker who had not even finished elementary school. Pa . . . believed that his actions preached bigger sermons than what he preached. It was a treat to ride with father as he made his visits in the parish. He always had time for his children. I only had him for 17 years of my life. People of the parish loved him as a friend possibly more so than as the pastor of the church. They knew he was not only a friend but one who would guide them to find help." Sigurd Urberg in a letter to the author, undated, September, 2000.

[22]Urberg's conservative theology did not preclude a radical stance on certain political issues. In 1894, just a year out of the Synod seminary, Urberg published an essay in his local newspaper in Norway in which he fully supported the railroad workers during the Pullman strike: "Fra Amerika," *Vestmar,* 31 July 1894.

[23]This information is given by H. G. Stub in "Nordre Beaver Creek menigheds historie," *Kirketidende,* 22 September 1909, 1044. N. F. S. Grundtvig's hymn has been translated into English as "God's Word Is Our Great Heritage." It is included in the contemporary *Lutheran Book of Worship* (Minneapolis and Philadelphia, 1978) as #239.

[24]From Urberg's sermon on Good Friday, 1911, given in the Ettrick church. The sermon is filed in a separate bundle entitled Easter sermons. On the last page of the handwritten manuscript Urberg records that he has used this particular sermon at least seven times, ending with Good Friday in the Trempealeau Valley Church in 1926. Søren S. Urberg's collection of sermons deserves a comprehensive study. In this essay I base my analysis on roughly 10% of the sermons in his file.

[25]Urberg's sermon on Good Friday, 1911.

[26]*"Også i vort gamle fædreland var forordnet ved kongebud, at den 4de fredag efter påske skulde være bods og bededag, og denne forordning har vi taget med hid til dette land."* Sermon in the Urberg file, preached at the Day of Penitence, *"bods og bededag,"* Trempealeau Valley Church, 1894. According to Urberg's notes this sermon was repeated at least ten times, the last time in Pine Creek in 1917.

[27]" . . . *vore landsmænds og vort lands synder.*" From Urberg's conclusion to the same sermon as in the previous footnote.

[28]"*. . . og som vi har bedet for at Gud vilde velsigne sæden på vore marker, og Gud har bønhørt os at vi fik en velsignet høst.*" Sermon on Thanksgiving Day, "*taksigelsesdagen,*" in 1899 in the Trempealeau Valley Church. According to Urberg's notes, this sermon was repeated at least seven times, the last time in Blair and Taylor in 1926. The text for the day was Psalm 34. The sermon is in the Urberg file.

[29]Karl Barth, *Homiletics,* trans. Geoffrey W. Bromiley and Donald E. Daniels (Louisville, KY, 1991), 119.

[30]"*Prædiken skal ikke gjøre os tilfreds med prædikanten, men den skal gjøre os utilfreds med os selv.*" See sermon cited in note 25. In this sermon Urberg emphasizes the difference in status between Paul, "the tent maker," and Felix, "the governor."

[31]*Skandinaven,* 23 May 1917.

[32]"*Født, døbt derborte mellem Norges fjelde, der blev hun i barndommen undervist i den lutherske lære, og i den lære blev [hun] bestyrket, ved sin konfirmation og den lutherske lære holdt hun fast ved til sin død, intet kunde drive hende fra sin fædrene kirke, det var hendes største hellige arv.*" Funeral sermon in the Urberg file, preached in Trempealeau Valley Church on 30 September 1907. Urberg's text on "a Sabbath rest for the people of God" is from Hebrews 4:9–11.

[33]"*Født, døbt, opvoxen og konfirmeret på den skandinaviske halvø . . . Men der havde han ikke nogen blivende stad, men ved Guds styrelse, drog han over det store verdens hav og fik sig et nyt hjem her på vestens store vidder, men ikke heller her fik han et blivende sted, men han måtte nedlægge sine trætte ben til den sidste hvile og ombytte den omvexlende tid med den uendelige evighed.*" This funeral sermon was first preached in Ettrick on 3 August 1904 and then repeated in Blair, 20 June 1907. In the Urberg file.

[34]". . . *han vil efter hans jordiske pilgrims vandring her nede, ved en rolig død, gå ud af landflygtigheden til det evige hjem, til det himmelske faderhus.*" See sermon in note 32.

[35]"*Hvor lidet er givet, skal lidet fordres.*" Same sermon as above.

[36]Funeral sermon for I. P. Stokke, 6 February 1897. The sermon is in the archives at Luther Theological Seminary, St. Paul, Minnesota.

37*"Vi ser 6 barn hvoraf 2 a 3 endnu ikke fatter det store tab, de har lidt."* Sermon in the Urberg file, dated 28 December 1928.

38Funeral sermon [*Gravtale*], 13 January 1897. The original is located in the archives at Luther Seminary, St. Paul, Minnesota.

39Sermon preached at the funeral of Syver Hjerleid, Trempealeau Valley Church, 2 March 1909. The sermon is in the Urberg file.

40All references in this paragraph are to a funeral sermon in the Urberg file based on 2 Timothy 4:4–7, which includes the well-known statement: "I have fought the good fight, I have finished the race, I have kept the faith." According to the information at the end of his manuscript, Urberg used the basic structure of this sermon at least eight times between 1900 and 1928.

41Unsigned and undated note, two small handwritten pages, tucked into Urberg's bundle of funeral sermons in his file.

42*"Bibelen, salmebogen var hans daglige læsning og jo ældre han blev desto mere glad blev han i dem. Og det er den rette vei, måtte også vi vandre på samme."* Funeral sermon dated 15 November 1927. It is in the Urberg file.

43Funeral sermon for a little child [*Gravtale over et lidet barn*], Beaver Creek Church, first delivered 27 April 1907. It is in the Urberg file.

Vignettes from a Norwegian-American Congregation: Urland Lutheran Church

Lloyd Hustvedt

ALONG THE WESTERN EDGE of the plat map for Leon Township in Goodhue County, Minnesota, a small cross, hardly visible, shows the location of Urland Lutheran Church, built in 1872. This congregation's first sin was to violate geographic fair play. Three of its four trustee districts lay to the west of the church. Those living in the western district chafed under this injustice for thirty years before they built their own church in 1908.

The first settlers had begun to move into this region eighteen years earlier. Some had helped Bernt Julius Muus build Holden Church. Urland came to be by a shearing off of Holden's northern-most trustee district, and a few grumbled against the Lord when they learned that they would have to do it all over again. The congregation began with 100 land-owning families and may have peaked with 118 in 1888.

About 85 percent of the members came from an overpopulated and for that reason an impoverished region in Inner Sogn called *"Aurland."* An entire community was transplanted. Leaving behind old prejudices, difficult neighbors, or your own past mischief was out of the question. Some farms in Aurland had multiple units. This explains why the congregation had an inordinate number of Flaams, Underdahls, Vangens, Otterneses, Ohnstads, and Fretheims. This church had to be named "Urland." A more global view came into play

Urland Lutheran Church

when an idyllic valley, two miles west of the church, got the name "Sogn." They pronounced it *Sågen.*

The people of Urland believed in God and they shared a common need for a church. For all that, religious expression ranged from sainthood to raw materialism. One of the Otterneses may have spoken for the majority. After listening to stories about the strange behavior of a pietist, he said, *"Eg æ no religiøs eg og, men eg fær no mæ' maute"* ["I am religious too, but I go at it with moderation"].

The constitution of the congregation declared that males should run it. The annual meeting fell on May 15, followed by a semiannual one in November. The minister served as chairman. The officers consisted of five trustees, one for each district, and a chief trustee who also served as treasurer. This organizational structure remained intact for sixty-five years until deacons were added in 1937. Alongside the constitution two unwritten laws functioned as the congregation's subconscious. The first: "The longer a practice exists the more right it seems that it should be so." The second: "The more impoverished the environment from which an emigrant came, the more frugal he or she tends to be in the new world." One *Aurlenning* did not let his children run if they had shoes on their feet on the theory that they wore out faster that way. The more frugal made for a majority at Urland and they determined fiscal policy. The less frugal, however, made for a feisty minority.

The budget item called *presteløn* [pastor's salary] held first priority. It actually covered the salaries of the minister, the *klokker* [precentor], the janitor, and later both the organist and the organ pumper. In the early days $350 per year was enough to cover these costs. Not until 1921 did this item exceed $1,000. Support for the larger church body, the Norwegian Synod, came second. It ranged from $180 to $200 per year and remained so until the merger in 1917. Maintenance of the church and the parsonage were cared for as needs arose. The first frivolous expenditure took place in 1897. The church treasury paid for the coffee and sugar consumed at the twenty-fifth anniversary celebration. The same recklessness was repeated twenty-five years later.

The concept of a general budget did not exist. If the church needed painting, or if the parsonage needed a new roof, the trustees walked the same miles and knocked on the same doors for each expenditure. So far did the practice of a decentralized budget go that communicants paid five cents each to cover the costs of the bread and wine. Not until 1910 did the church treasury pick up this expense. As early as 1887 a member argued against the folly of having a subscription for every expense. Nothing changed. The parishioners wanted to know to what they were giving. If a trustee solicited two causes simultaneously, they tended to give to one.

The more generous folk in the parish carried a disproportionate share of the financial burdens. In order to correct these inequities, the congregation adopted in 1889 a system called *ligning*, best translated as "apportionment." Based on net worth, families fell into one of four classes where the levies ranged from $7.75 at the top to $2.25 at the bottom. If you owned 160 acres or more you were in the first category. The plan was later refined to include seven classes, with an assessment of $8 at the top, and $.50 at the bottom. The names of delinquents were made public and they risked dismissal from the congregation, but curiously enough they could not themselves withdraw from the church without having first paid their back dues. *Ligning* was still in effect in 1933, but then it was back to four categories: a neat $16, $12, $9, and $6 plan.

Nothing disturbed the ministers who served Urland more than the congregation's refusal to make the parochial school a congregational responsibility. Without a well-run parochial school, they warned, the congregation would disintegrate. Pastor John Nathan Kildahl (1857–1920) noted that the Germans had it right. They found a teacher first and a minister second. The children in Madagascar, he said, have better schools than do the children of Urland. The parochial school had started as a do-it-yourself, district enterprise in the congregation. Parents hired their own teacher. The problem concerned coverage, not quality. For some children the walking distance was too great. Poor parents, certainly those with many children, could not afford the per-pupil cost. Indifferent parents could do as they pleased. Beginning at the turn of the century, Pastor Anders Hauge (1853–1931) often announced that children were reporting to him for confirmation who could not read Norwegian; some could not even recite the Lord's Prayer. Repeatedly, committees presented excellent plans that collapsed because the congregation refused to adopt the first proposition, namely, that the parochial school should be the responsibility of the congregation. Shame may have forced the adoption of a well-conceived plan in 1910. The congregation and the parents would share the costs equally. When this 50/50 provision was repealed the following year, the burden again fell back on dedicated parents and schoolteachers. Not until the mid-1930s did Urland establish a twenty-day summer English language parochial school with the congregation covering 75 percent of the costs.

The need for church-sponsored local charity was considerably diminished because the culture was such that neighbor helped neighbor. The people of Urland found it much easier to share their potato bins than their pocketbooks. Frequent appeals for help from the outside competed with domestic charity. Collections were made for the victims of grasshopper plagues, forest fire, and other disasters. Offerings on confirmation day were generally allocated to orphanages, to needy college students, to retired ministers, or to their widows. Some laudable measures took place on the local level. The single Swede in the congregation disappeared in 1897. A committee was formed to try to find him, and one person was instructed to visit, at congregational expense, places to which he might have gone. A girl threatened with blindness was sent to a Minneapolis doctor. In 1907, the church bought an invalid chair that later went out on loan to anyone that needed one. Only one hardship case induced a Sunday offering. It concerned a man named Eide, ruled "in need of help." A committee was formed in 1908 to look into poverty cases within the congregation, but there is no later reporting. In 1894 Knut Brekke's obligation to the church was reduced by 50 percent because hail had destroyed his grain crop. During the depression years, the congregation collected farm produce for the Ebenezer Home: potatoes, carrots, beets, onions, turnips, squash, and winter apples were delivered to the collection center. I remember questioning as a youngster the charitable merits of a heaping bushel basket of horseradish. One root alone was enough to burn out 100 stomachs. Not all appeals for help were honored. In 1919 Botolf Vangen hoped to go to the Ebenezer Home. A single payment of $1,000 was needed, but he had only $200. Would the parish raise the balance? Issues such as this were never rejected, only tabled. When the matter came up six months later, Botolf had been sent to the county poor farm.

Norway celebrated the centennial of its Constitution in 1914. Urland was invited to participate in a gift. With apologies to our

Norwegian friends, I quote the minutes: *"Men efter en del diskusjon, gikk man bort fra sagen"* ["After considerable discussion, the issue was dropped"]. Today Urland has a funded program entitled "Project Good Neighbor."

The so-called Election Controversy that tore apart the Norwegian Synod and split many of its congregations was, by contrast, a painless affair at Urland. The congregation followed the lead of its minister, J. N. Kildahl, an Anti-Missourian. The whole controversy began with church politics. Many members felt that F. A. Schmidt had been treated shabbily when denied a seat and speaking rights at a Synod convention. The congregation took a straw vote in 1883 on the proposition that "we regard the Synod we joined as no longer in existence." Fifty-four voted yes and four abstained. Four years later, when the Synod refused to recognize the new seminary at St. Olaf College in 1887, the congregation had to act. A motion to withdraw from the Synod passed without friction; fifty-five voted for this, three abstained, and one voted against it.

During my childhood and youth, church services ranged in number from twenty-four to twenty-eight per year. Services every other Sunday heightened the significance of *midden søndag*. The term *"midden,"* derived from the English word "meeting," had replaced *Gudstjeneste* [divine worship]. Working on Sunday was a greater sin than not attending church. Threshing rigs also stood still during the hours of a funeral. Threshing crews might line the road with straw hats in hand when the procession went by. Four to five communions per year attracted thirty to forty participants for an estimated annual total of 120. Communion involved two trips to the altar, the first for absolution with a laying on of hands, and the second for the bread and wine. Women wore hats to church but removed them for communion. This sacrament separated, but amiably so, the devout from the truly devout. Group identity entered as a factor. Going or not going to communion could entail peer loyalty or disloyalty if one broke ranks.

On the whole the Urland folk were theologically savvy. But, among some, folk beliefs had penetrated communion doctrine. One distortion may have been caused by ministers who stressed too much the sin of going unprepared to the Lord's table, even suggesting that this might be the unpardonable sin. Communion was risky business. One could be worse off going than not going. Some held the curious view that God dispensed, as it were, two kinds of forgiveness. One was the general, everyday kind. The second was a special gift-wrapped type that came only through communion. A gasoline-station theology took form. One of God's pumps dispensed regular, another high-test ethyl. In my day, more than half of Urland ran their spiritual engines on regular.

Church discipline, called *"kirketukt,"* was a serious matter. I mention some representative cases. In 1877, Ole Hagen was called on the carpet for permitting dancing and drinking in his home. He promised to mend his ways. Later two of his sons were investigated for possible connections with the Freemasons. In the same year, a Mali Sachariasdatter confessed to praising false doctrine and that she had in other ways shown scorn for her faith. She was forgiven. If this was a heresy case, it was the only one. The messiest were marriage misalliance cases, often involving wives who had left their husbands. As a rule, wives cited brutality as a cause. In one instance a couple had been reconciled by agreeing to a divorce. The congregation sent word to the husband that reconciliation under such terms went contrary to Scripture. His wife was summoned. She answered yes to a number of cited sins, but when asked if she had sinned when she left her husband without his permission, she hesitated and just said, "Perhaps." She was found inadequately contrite. A woman named Herborg stated that only in risking her life could she return to her husband. The congregation could do with her as it pleased. It did nothing.

Women who gave birth outside of wedlock led the way in numbers of cases. Appearing before an assembly of fifty or more men was hardly pleasant, but the ritual was brief. Had she sinned when she committed adultery and gave secret birth? "Yes." Did she beg the congregation's forgiveness for the scandal her sin had caused? "Yes." Did she promise improved behavior in the future? "Yes." Kindhearted Atle Flom could be counted on to move instantly for forgiveness which, with rare exceptions, was granted. A few chose excommunication rather than appear. There were three in 1917. Only once, in 1910, was the father summoned and his name revealed. He refused to appear.

One case concerned a young man who left the farm and took over a saloon in Cannon Falls. One painful and protracted case involved a man who stole wheat from his neighbor. Mons Stondal, never comfortable at *kirketukt*, argued unsuccessfully for not recording disciplinary cases in the minutes.

This dreary parade of human judgment offered moments of comic relief. At a church meeting in 1895, Knut Esterby rose to report that Ole Flom had called him a liar. This reckless act had taken place at the annual meeting of District School No. 52. Knut said that he had lived up to the requirements of Matthew 18:15-17, but Ole still refused to retract his words. Ole was not present at the time so judgment had to wait. At the next meeting, Ole said that he had not exactly called Knut a liar. But, when Knut had grossly exaggerated the distance between the schoolhouse and a certain point to the north, he could not help but remind Knut that it was not nice of him not to tell the truth. One person suggested that this could be settled by taking a physical measurement of the distance in question. But the issue now involved ethical implications that transcended any scientific solution. That remarkable minister, Carl Gustav Mellby (1869-1940) presided over this meeting. Sensing, perhaps, that the passion tanks were near empty, Mellby in his wisdom did not ask Ole to retract his words, but rather: "Ole, will you shake hands with Knut." Ole said that he would.

Church discipline lost its will to live and died quietly around 1920, and now lies in an unmarked grave. The final case, a tragicomic affair, ran from 1915 to 1919. It began as follows: Pastor Anders Hauge announced in 1915 that he wished to dispel the rumor that he had refused to baptize a child born out of wedlock. Seeing it as a ploy to avert discipline he had, however, refused a request for home baptism. Two men visited the mother, whose name was Ingeborg. She agreed to appear on the condition that others in similar circumstances were summoned. These men asked the minister to perform home baptism, which he did. A new delegation now went to see Ingeborg, but she now refused unconditionally to appear. When she was about to be dropped from the church roster, what had been suspected became known. Her father, Peder, had forbidden his daughter to appear. Now both father and daughter were summoned, and two of Urland's finest men were appointed to reason with Peder. When they arrived, Peder told them that he had become tired of these church visits and that he wanted no more of them. A year later a rumor surfaced that Peder had undergone a change of heart and that he wanted to talk with the minister. When the minister called, Peder assured him that there was no truth in the rumor. At the annual meeting of 1919, Peder was declared *selvavsatt* [self-ousted].

At this meeting another problem arose. No one would take on the job of janitor. The duties had mounted over time, and the salary was $90 a year. A committee of two was appointed scrounge up a janitor. With no intervening explanation, we learn from the minutes of a meeting six months later that the janitor they found was none other than our troublesome Peder, and that his salary had been elevated to a staggering $100. On the folk level, two views on church discipline divided the congregation. Some saw it as an instrument of love meant to edify a wayward Christian. Others regarded it as punishment for sins committed.

Odd Otternes was born in Aurland in 1840 and emigrated in 1857, and from that time on he worked tirelessly at becoming Urland's most difficult citizen. Few have harbored a more lofty disdain for public opinion than he. Had the poet John Donne known him, Donne would not have written the words "No man is an island." Odd was intelligent and at times quite right about things. This only compounded the problem. The dynamics of this man's presence defy measurement. When a proposal to install a pipe organ first came up in 1887, he reminded the assembly that the church needed painting. When the proposal came up to paint the church, he argued that this could wait until next year. Once the church was painted, the matter of an organ resurfaced. Odd then reminded the congregation that on top of the initial cost of an organ, they would have to hire an organist, and that organists did not come cheap. After twenty-one years, Urland got its pipe organ in 1908. It was Odd who came up with the apportionment plan, but later railed against it for its many injustices. He had an uncanny nose for sniffing out disciplinary cases and could be the single holdout on a motion to forgive. This created a problem for Pastor J. N. Kildahl, who believed that congregational forgiveness was worthless if not unanimous. Kildahl once denied Odd future speaking rights until he recanted. As early as 1888, Odd argued that there would be no sense to the parochial school system unless they went over to the English language. It will come, said Kildahl, but not just yet.

At an 1882 meeting, Odd spoke as follows: "I maintain that the motion I presented at the last meeting, which was seconded and which the chairman ruled out of order, was valid. Such action by the chairman makes it clear that he has transgressed the laws of God and those of our nation."

Lars Flom rose and asked, "How long are we going to tolerate these crass remarks from Odd Otternes?"

The pastor responded: "I make it a point not to pay any attention to what Odd Otternes says. I am convinced that he is no longer in control of his choice of words."

Twenty-four years later Odd raised the ante. He accused Pastor Hauge of having sinned against God, against the congregation, and against the laws of Minnesota. Now Odd had gone too far. A special meeting was called for 1 February 1906. The president and vice president of the church, the district president, and the president of St. Olaf College, J. N. Kildahl, were invited to serve as a jury and render a verdict. The person found to be in the wrong would pay the costs. Only Vice President Ellestad came. But on that day the battleship Otternes took a torpedo right in the engine room and began to sink. It went down, however, with all its flags flying.

The tradition of giving names to farm animals lived on in our settlement. The cows had Norwegian names like Lykkebot, Rosa, and Litagod because cows never left the farm and the farm was Norwegian. In contrast, I never met a Norwegian horse. They sported aristocratic names like King, Queen, Prince, Duke, and Colonel. But there were lower-class names, too, like Daisy, Belle, Dolly, Lady, Betsy, Nelly,

Jack, Jim, and Charley. Horses had Anglican names because they went to town, and towns were American. It was, of course, only a matter of time before the children of Urland would go the way of the horse. It began timidly. In 1882 a child in Urland was baptized Henry, not Henrik. Six years later, in 1888, came a second Henry. In 1891 the congregation heard at baptism the name Angelo Sacharias Ingemann Tveitmo. Angelo was the name of the emigrant ship that had transported this child's father to America. In 1893 came a "Gertie." The name was already in use as an anglicized version of Gjertrude. The first Robert and the first Lewis appeared in 1895. A number of Lars's had before this time adopted the name Lewis. The year 1896 marks a clean break with the past. Three baby girls were given the name Mabel. Before the century ended there were three more Mabels, another Henry, and an exotic Chester Alonzo. The pace picked up astonishing momentum at the turn of the century. By 1903 we had multiples of names like Pearl, Ruby, Myrtle, Hazel, and Gladys. Early on, Myron, Clarence, Obert, Ember, Elmer, Harry, and Arthur were popular masculine names. Save for coming up with new and more exotic names, the transition was complete by 1916. The baptism of a child named Beula took an unfortunate turn. The minister had misheard the sponsor and spoke as follows: "Mula, I baptize Thee. . . ." Discussions followed as to how binding was God's version of this name.

The Reverend Anders Hauge served Urland from 1898 to 1925. He presided over the alpha and omega of this cultural disaster. I can imagine him asking at each baptism: "Oh, where, oh, where have all the Rognalds and Ragnhilds gone? Gone to horse names every one." He pleaded with his congregation. They were giving names to their children, he said, that were not names. If they were names at all, they were names void of tradition and meaning. On the surface everything else in the community remained Norwegian. In fact, the congregation sent strongly worded resolutions to church headquarters declaring their opposition to dropping the word "Norwegian" from the name of the church.

An anecdote documents how entrenched things had become by 1908. Anders and Ragnhilda Indrelie were more recent immigrants.

They could speak no English. When they brought twins to church for baptism and declared that their names were to be "Pete and Lewis," the minister urged strongly that for the records, at least, the names be "Peder and Lars." Anders responded defiantly in his finest *Sogning* dialect: *"Vitkje presten doipa dai Pete og Lewis, so tæk eg dei ti Cannon Falls og doipa dei dar"* ["If the minister will not baptize them as Pete and Lewis, I will have them baptized in Cannon Falls"]. When I examined the baptismal records I uncovered a stirring fact. Pastor Hauge had entered correctly in his exquisite hand the name Lewis but by force of habit, he had then written the name Peter, only later to draw a neat line through the letter "r" so as to create the name "Pete."

Urland's pioneer lore concerned both clergy and laity. We cite a sample from each. Carl Gustav Mellby came to the parish fresh from the seminary—youthful, handsome, and athletic. During confirmation recess he coached strapping farm lads in the arts of wrestling, making sure that he pinned each one in turn. To this one *Sogning* commented, "You have dynamite when you mix God's Word with wrestling skills." Mellby was an avid reader. When he left his parsonage and came to a certain fork in the road, his horse knew to which church they were going. Mellby then tied up his reins, pulled out a book, and from that time on he was lost to the external world. Along the way farm families dropped their work to gaze upon their reading minister who moved down the road with a horse on automatic pilot. The pulpit at Urland was adorned with a fringe of twisted golden threads with tiny tufts at the end. During his sermon, Mellby, moving left to right, would lay one strand after the other on the velvet cushion on the pulpit railing. When he missed a strand, a collective prayer would go up for this orphan. At an emphatic point in his sermon, he could with a single sweep of his right hand undo his handiwork, only to start over again. Sisyphus had come to Urland. After church services Mellby watered his horse at a nearby farmstead. The windows were set high in the church; only from the pulpit could one see what passed by on the road. One Sunday, toward the end of his sermon, Mellby saw his horse and carriage trot by without a driver. His horse had loosed itself and was on its way to water. To an astonished congregation, Mellby interrupted his sermon and announced: "My horse has just informed me that today my sermon is much too long. The *kirkesanger* [precentor] will give the closing prayer." In the records for the following congregational meeting, you will find a resolution declaring that the janitor will from this date on care for the minister's horse. Mellby left in 1897 to study in Germany. Upon his return, he joined the faculty at St. Olaf College.

A woman named Anna ranks high in local lore. She was the daughter of the first settler in Leon Township and no member of the DAR could have been more proud. She was asked to move one Sunday because she sat in a pew set aside for visiting dignitaries. She was so offended at this that she took a mighty vow never again to set foot inside her church as long as she lived. About thirty years later an unfortunate thing happened. Her husband died. On everybody's lips was the question: Would Anna attend her husband's funeral? Some felt that it would be a sign of weakness if she did. Moderates argued that there were limits to how long pledges like hers had a right to endure. Anna did not attend her husband's funeral. Some years later, Anna, too, died and then she came to church. It was a large funeral.

I have been told that the practice of having women sit on the left-hand side of the church and men on the right had its origin in convenience. Men dropped off women and children before they tied up their horses. On the way in they visited with neighbors, exchanged seed grains, or bartered a pig for a calf. They entered often as a group when the bell rang. Congestion was avoided by giving men their own space. The truth hardly matters. Tradition had made it God's will. Its downfall came about as follows. Not far from the church lived a young man named Clarence. In a fight with his brothers, he always got the worst of it. Hoping to reverse this role, he did his first most unheard-of thing: he joined the U.S. Marines. Community opinion at the time was that only those who wanted to lead immoral lives without their neighbors knowing about it joined the military. He came home when his stint was over, but his brothers still overpowered him. He married and moved out of the community, but then some years later he bought a farm near the church. It was then that he did his second most unheard-of thing: He came to church and sat with his wife on the left-hand side. I was in church that historic day. The expression "not knowing whether to laugh or cry" fits: one-half of the congregation laughed; the other half cried. Not until I entered military service during World War II did I realize that Clarence had carried out a classic marine maneuver. First you invade, then you establish a beachhead, and then you just hang in there until more help arrives.

The *kirkesanger* or *klokker* spoke for the congregation. The opening and closing prayers were his to speak because they opened with the words, "*We* [meaning the congregation] gather in Thy presence to hear Thy holy Word. . . ." and "*We* render unto Thee our heartfelt thanks. . . ." Urland had only two *kirkesangere*. The first served from 1872 to 1879. The second and last, Iver Davidson Hustvedt, held that office from 1879 to 1910. He also served as recording secretary for thirty-three years and taught parochial school in the parish for forty years. His beginning *klokker* salary of $25 per year had climbed to $40 by 1908. In that year the congregation raised his salary to $70. This happened in the same year the congregation installed a pipe organ. At the 1910 meeting, a staunch frugalist moved that they do away with the *klokker* position, arguing that the congregation could not possibly support both a *klokker* and an organist. A counter-proposal that they retain the position but reduce the salary to $30 passed, but with the rider that for the time being they would do without. None was later appointed.

The rite of purification after childbirth for *inngangskoner* [the "churching" of women returning to church for the first time after giving birth] survived the *klokker* tradition, but this too before long vanished. A motion making the churching of women optional was passed on 15 May 1916. As far as I know, no one opted to follow this practice again.

Women tended their own vineyard. The Ladies Aid stood by as a rescue operation, often picking up residual debts the men found difficult to pay. They also did fine things for interior esthetic improvement. Women were first appointed to committees during World War

I. This was related to work for the Red Cross. Later came Sunday School assignments. By the mid-1930s women dominated committees and boards that concerned church education. Old attitudes held firm regarding franchise. A resolution granting women the right to vote first came up in 1949. It was at this troublesome meeting that the sage of Leon Township saved the day with humor and reverse psychology. He declared that he firmly believed that women should have the right to vote, but he could not for the world get himself to believe that they should have it right now. Six months later, in 1950, the tabled resolution granting franchise to women passed without discussion. The current president of Urland is a woman.

The minutes from 1940 to 1945 are missing. But within these years church meetings went from being conducted in Norwegian to English. We hear a toot from Gabriel's horn on 8 November 1939. Though conducted in Norwegian, the meeting on that date opened with singing hymn No. 18 from the English hymnal. Taking confirmation in English first became an option in 1919. In a 1936 class of seven, I was one of two taking confirmation in Norwegian. My sister was the last one to do so in 1937. Confirmation moved from being all Norwegian to being all English in a matter of eighteen years.

Confirmation was a rigorous two-year affair. We memorized everything. Confirmation day meant public catechization. Studies for confirmation marked my first contact with an intellectual. I marveled at the minister's capacity to explain words in terms of their Greek, Latin, and at times Hebrew origins. I felt that I had an edge on my English colleagues. For a fourteen-year-old *helliggjørelse* is easier to grasp than "sanctification"; *innblest* and *omvendelse* are more self-descriptive than are "inspired" and "conversion."

The minutes of Urland are written in flawless Norwegian up until 1910, with a penmanship to match. These thorough and precise records often include direct discourse and are free of the English intrusions that characterized the oral speech of the day. The quality of Norwegian in the later minutes remains excellent, but with some loss in penmanship and in precision. In contrast, the switch from Norwegian to English reveals a pronounced reduction in quality. One finds awkward sentences and misspelled words. When the term "synod" is spelled "cinod," one finds new arguments for the return of church discipline. The English records lack the sense for history that permeated the earlier Norwegian ones.

The spring cleaning of the cemetery, attended mainly by men and their sons old enough to manage a rake or a shovel, was a rite of brotherhood. I recall with pleasure how my father and the men about him enjoyed each other. Good will and harmony prevailed when the men of Urland worked side by side. As far as I can recall, this was the only official church event that did not require the presence of the minister.

For an entertainment-starved congregation, the church-sponsored summer evening "Ice Cream Socials" were a blessing for the youth of the congregation. The finest farmsteads were chosen, but a front porch and a well-kept lawn were the only things needed. After a program and a short sermon, the teenagers began their Lutheran-approved dancing on the green. One dance was "The farmer's dog lay on the barn floor and Bingo was his name." Boys and girls sashayed in opposite directions as they spelled out B I N G O. The stop at "O" marked your new temporary partner. Another was "Jerry the Miller who lived by the mill." Later came these curious sentences: "With a hand in the hopper and the other in the sack. The ladies go forward and gents turn back." This was Urland rock-and-roll. Future marriages were made at these games. It began with a knowing squeeze of the hand. If there was a similar squeeze in return, it could lead straight to the altar. This is Norwegian love.

A few random remarks. Oil lamps were installed twelve years after founding, thus making evening meetings possible. These were replaced with gas lamps in 1923. Rural electrification came through ten years later. A pesky problem found a solution in 1893: signs were posted in the entryway, forbidding the spitting of tobacco in church. The first Christmas tree program, sponsored by the youth organization, took place in 1896. This annual event marked for most children their first, and often terrifying, public appearance. The Madagascar missionary Christian Borchgrevink and the Santal missionary Lars Skrefsrud were rated the most famous persons to visit the congregation during its first fifty years. The new practice of leaving the grave before it was filled was resolutely rejected in 1903. In 1906 Pastor Hauge asked the congregation to rule on a prolonged rift between himself and Ole Hagen. He said he would accept whatever the congregation decided. A telephone was installed in the parsonage in 1908, but it never worked. In 1928 the church was raised two and one-half feet in order to make a modern social and educational center in the basement. As a measure to help pay for the costs of this renovation, the first *lutefisk* supper came to be. The supper rose out of economic necessity but proved to be so popular that it became an annual affair. The minister's salary went from $1,500 to $1,800 in 1936. The organ was equipped with an electric blower in 1937, and the organ pumper lost his job. In that same year the church bought its very first fire extinguisher. We have no explanation for this sudden loss of faith.

Suddenly in the early 1940s teenagers from Urland began to attend high school, most of them in Cannon Falls. These innocents not only socialized with Cannon Falls Yankees, Swedes, and other ethnics. They began to marry them. The Urland Norwegian empire began to crumble and nothing has made much sense after that.

From 1880 to 1993, a period of 113 years, Urland saw an average of 12 baptisms per year with a high of 32 in 1883. Confirmation classes averaged 11 per year, with a high of 31 in 1886. Funerals averaged 7 per year with a high of 18 in 1900. Weddings have run about 3 per year with a high of 9 in 1970.

Urland remains a viable congregation today with 360 confirmed members. Many live and work in nearby towns. Only two farms have dairy cattle. The names of the families that have joined Urland in recent years tell of a new age: Soul, Cole, Chapman, Theim, Weibel, Reinke, Slevin, Landry, Kuhl, Rechtzigel, Van Guilder, McWaters,

Baisch, Hugget, and one is symbolically named Welcome. The minister's name is McLaughlin. The church is run by an intricate mix of trustees, deacons, officers, boards, committees, and managers. One meeting a year is now adequate because it functions more as a channel for communication between the committees and membership than as a deliberating body in the old sense. There is worship every Sunday with communion twice a month. The current annual budget has tripled over the past twenty years. It now stands at about $100,000. During the past ten years there has been an average of nine baptisms per year, 6 students in each confirmation class, and five funerals and weddings annually.

Lutherans, as I understand it, do not have a precise doctrine on what transpires between death and the resurrection. But at the many Urland funerals I have attended, kind ministers have strongly hinted that the people of whom I have written here have already passed muster. Given my biases in the matter, I hope it is true.

The Authors

JON GJERDE is Professor of History at the University of California at Berkeley. He has recently published *The Minds of the West: Ethnocultural Evolution in the Rural Middle West, 1830-1917* (1997) and *Major Problems in American Ethnic and Immigration History* (1998). Gjerde is editor of the Statue of Liberty—Ellis Island Centennial Series.

ØYVIND T. GULLIKSEN is Associate Professor of American Literature and Culture, Telemark College, Bø i Telemark. He has recently published a number of studies including *Double Landscapes—Midwestern Texts: Studies in Norwegian-American Literature* (1999).

VIDAR L. HAANES is Professor of Church History at the Norwegian Lutheran School of Theology—Oslo (*Menighetsfakultetet*). Among his publications is *Hvad skal da dette blive for prester?* (1998), which deals with Norwegian and Norwegian-American pastoral training from a transatlantic perspective.

LLOYD HUSTVEDT is Emeritus Professor of Norwegian at Saint Olaf College, Northfield, Minnesota and the retired Executive Secretary of the Norwegian-American Historical Association. He is the author of *Rasmus Bjørn Anderson* (1966) and a number of other studies in Norwegian-American history.

MARION JOHN NELSON was Emeritus Professor at the University of Minnesota. Nelson was also author of numerous publications on the art and material culture of Norwegian-Americans. Among his recent publications is *Norwegian Folk Art: The Migration of a Tradition* (1995).

ORM ØVERLAND is Professor of American Literature at the University of Bergen. Among his books are *Johan Schrøder's Travels in Canada, 1863* (1989), *The Western Home: A Literary History of Norwegian America* (1996), and *Immigrant Minds, American Identities: Making the United States Home, 1870-1930* (2000).

BJØRN SANDVIK is Pastor of Bryn Congregation in Bærum, Diocese of Oslo. A former Research Associate of the Church of Norway Research center in Oslo, he is the author of *Det store nattverdfallet* (1998), a study of communion practices in both Norway and Norwegian America during the period of immigration.

KATHLEEN STOKKER is Professor of Norwegian at Luther College. She has recently published *Folklore Fights the Nazis: Humor in Occupied Norway, 1940-1945* (1995) and *Keeping Christmas: Yuletide Traditions in Norway and the New Land* (2000).